CW00833555

RECESSION-PROOF
FOR BEGINNERS

BEAR MARKET INVESTING STRATEGIES
WITH DIVIDEND, IPOs,
INVERSE ETFs & SHORT SELLING

WILL WEISER

Disclaimer

Every effort was made to produce this book as truthful as possible, but no warranty is implied. The author shall have neither liability nor responsibility to any person or entity concerning any loss or damages ascending from the information contained in this book. The information in the following pages are broadly considered to be truthful and accurate of facts, and such any negligence, use or misuse of the information in question by the reader will render any resulting actions solely under their purview.

Table of Contents

Introduction

If you want to discover how to survive the bear market, this book is for you. Everyone can become wealthy on a bull market but if you want to discover how to thrive on the bear market and want to discover how to profit from THE GREAT RESET, you will find this book extremely useful. First you will discover what are the best inflation proof assets to protect your wealth. Next you will discover how to use several bear market strategies such as dollar cost averaging, dividend investing, short selling, wheel options strategy and inverse ETF investing. After that, you will learn what are the best recession-proof stocks that you should invest before the bear market. Next, you will discover how to predict recession using inverted yield curve and how to research stocks using fundamental analysis. Lastly, you will learn how and where to invest successfully in IPOs or Initial Public Offerings. If you are ready to change your life and multiply your wealth, let's first cover how to profit from THE GREAT RESET!

Chapter 1 How To Profit From The Great Reset

Before we talk about different ways to profit from the Great Reset, let's take a step back and talk about what exactly that is. The Great Reset is a term that has been tossed around over the last few years. As far as the origin it came from the 50th annual meeting of the World Economic Forum in 2020. Essentially this is a large group of thought leaders and different individuals in charge of large countries coming together to figure out how to navigate The New Normal. There is an official plan for the Great Reset which you can look at yourself, but it breaks it down into three different components. Number one is to create more of a stakeholder economy. Number two is emphasis on ESG going forward with our investments and then number three is harnessing Innovations from the fourth Industrial Revolution. If you don't know what some or any of that is, don't worry we're going to cover all of it in just a little bit. For now we'll just explain the fourth Industrial Revolution. What that means is the rapid changes in technology, industry as well as societal patterns due to increasing interconnectivity and smart automation. Now you understand what the Great Reset is. It's this big economic plan where there are tons of very large countries involved. Now let's talk about how you could potentially profit from the Great Reset. The very first investment vehicle to potentially profit from the Great Reset is called I Bonds. You may have never heard of these before and that's because inflation isn't really something we've had to combat in the past. But now that inflation is so high, a lot of people are looking for ways to essentially protect their savings in the buying power of their money, so one thing that you could do here is put your cash reserve on ice, or at least some of it allowing you to hopefully outpace inflation - essentially earmarking those funds for a later date. That could mean investing in stocks, crypto, real estate, all sorts of different things, but if you don't plan on investing just yet putting your money on ice and making sure you're outpacing inflation could be a very solid choice. If you're anything like me, you probably have the tendency to buy the dip a little bit too quickly on different Investments. This could also be an option to essentially protect you from you and make it so you can't just throw your money right back into the market, and with inflation running above 8% as we mentioned people are very worried about this deterioration of their buying power. What a lot of people have done is just blindly thrown their money into the stock or crypto Market to try to outpace inflation, but if you look at the year-to-date performance on both, that would have lost you a lot more money than the simple loss from inflation. Since blindly throwing your money into the market isn't a great strategy, this could be a solid alternative, keeping your money on ice. The full name of this investment vehicle is the Series I Savings Bond and there's two different rates that are important to be familiar with. The first one is the fixed rate which stays the same for the life of the bond. The important one is the second rate which is the inflation rate which is set two times annually and it's based on the CPI or Consumer Price Index, aka the indicator we use to track inflation. Right now, that six month rate is at 9.62% on a bond guaranteed by the US Government. This certainly sounds like a great deal but there are a few caveats to be aware of before you get super excited about this. First of all, you can only invest ten thousand dollars per year in I Bonds per Social Security number, so if you have $10,000 or less of an emergency fund or money that you're earmarking for later investment you could be in good shape here to utilize these I Bonds. If you have two hundred thousand dollars in cash, putting ten thousand dollars into this product really might not be worth it for you in terms of the fact that the other $190,000 that you have is still sitting in a Bank account or somewhere where it's not keeping up with inflation. The second thing to be aware of is that you can hold on to these I Bonds until maturity or you can sell them early in the secondary Market.

The only thing is if you do sell them early before maturity, you do forfeit the last three months of interest that you earned. Let's say for example you didn't want to put your money into the markets right now, but you wanted to protect yourself from inflation. You could theoretically put ten thousand into the I Bonds, fully maxing it out for the year and then over the next 12 months earned that interest rate and it's going to be right now 9.62% and then it's going to be recalculated later on this year. Assuming one year later you decided to redeem those bonds, you would lose three months of that interest so you would have earned nine months instead of 12 full months of that interest. Even so, this is still the best place to park ten thousand dollars right now, fully insured and backed by the US Government. However it just might not be worthwhile for those that have a gigantic cash nest egg that they're looking to protect the buying power of. So strategy number one just to recap is protecting yourself from inflation via I Bonds, while you essentially let the Great Reset play out which could lead to tremendous buying opportunities across different Financial assets.

The second idea to profit from the Great Reset that is to invest in Innovation. Before you go out there and start blindly throwing your money into crypto and Innovation stocks just like crashy wood, pump the brakes for a minute because obviously doing this without a defined strategy or doing it too early could have disastrous results. So before we talk about Innovation, we need to recap and talk about the last economic crisis in 2020. The 2020 stock market crash ended up being a flash in the pan with an Abrupt v-shaped recovery, largely based on record monetary policy, and as we now know this in turn set off the Great Reset. Based on this current record inflation we are seeing, the FED is expected to aggressively tighten interest rates for the rest of 2020. This among other factors has caused the biggest crypto drawdown in recent memory as well as a nasty sell-off in both growth and speculative stock. All that being said, it's important to keep in mind that Apple and Amazon stock both crashed during the.com bubble in the early 2000s, however if you somehow had the insight to buy those stocks at that time, your return you would have had would have been absolutely unbelievable. So if you have a defined process for researching Investments and finding value, coming up in the next 12 to 24 months let's say, could be one of the biggest opportunities to invest in Innovation at some of the best prices in the last few decades. That being said, we are going to see a lot of companies get completely washed out because they were probably operating businesses that would never ordinarily be sustainable in a higher interest rate environment.

You could even invest in cryptocurrencies as a method of investing in future Innovation, however just bear in mind right now that the very use case for most cryptocurrencies is being challenged right now. For example over the last few years I don't know how many different times I heard people say that Bitcoin was a logical hedge against inflation. Well, if we've learned anything in 2022, it is that that is one hundred percent not the case. But that being said investing in Innovation slowly and with a defined strategy could be a way to capitalize on one of the goals of the Great Reset. My advice is simply to be patient learn and move slowly, because although Innovation happens quickly, people tend to very much over price these things today. For example if you were FOMOing into crypto in 2021 had you held off you would be getting much better prices today.

The third and final way to profit from the Great Reset is to start a business. One of the biggest lessons that the last few years has taught all of us is that certainty has gone completely out of the window. In the past most people stick with the job that they may not like for whatever reason for that stability, however a lot of young people are learning that that stability is just not guaranteed or something that could be relied on today. So instead of working in a job that you don't like without stability, a lot of people are making the decision to start a side hustle and then maybe even transition into that as a full-time business, once things are getting off the ground. In this 1099 Revolution or work from home movement has essentially opened up an entirely different category for Savvy individuals who want to make money without working in a traditional job, and so what I have found is that times of disruption are usually the best times looking back to have started a business and that is largely because everything around you is changing largely at the same time. With so much changing quickly and all of these new resources available, it's possible to build and scale a business very quickly in 2022. So perhaps this may be the time to make that investment in yourself and potentially long punch that side hustle or business idea. If you don't quite know what you want to do yet, study those very people who have figured out how to work from home or start their own 1099 business and then you can simply mirror those same strategies.

Chapter 2 Best Inflation Proof Assets to Protect Your Wealth

Unless you've been living under a rock we've all been hearing about this rampant inflation that is pretty much hurting us in all areas of life. If you are trying to not have it hurt your portfolio so much, we're going to be covering the top six inflation proof investments. But before we get into the actual investments, let's start by talking more about inflation because a lot of people don't know as much about inflation as they think and the reason is because for most of us including myself for the majority of my life, inflation really hasn't been a concern because it's been in this normal target figure of roughly 2% annually. The Central Bank targets healthy inflation of roughly 2% annually, so right off the bat no not all inflation is bad in fact a little bit of inflation indicates a healthy and normally functioning economy. Inflation is that general increase of prices and services over time. Now we understand the what behind inflation, let's get into the causes. Number one we have cost push inflation. This is what we're experiencing right now, which is where increasing production costs are pushing prices up. Think about things like fuel costs, raw materials etc., cost push inflation comes from just these overall increasing costs associated with production and then also transportation of different goods. Earlier in 2021 we experienced the other type of inflation which is demand pull inflation. This is when you have rising consumer demand which means you have high demand for goods and services, pushing prices up. You have two different types of inflation that we have already seen, but there's a third which is Government policy inflation which comes from changing interest rates, adjusting tax rates and increasing the money supply. Of course we had record money printing going on in 2020 during the global pandemic and that's what led to a lot of that demand pull inflation that we saw in 2021 and now in 2022 with all of these supply chain issues and different things going on, we're now experiencing cost push inflation. What is the impact? Well I probably don't have to tell most people because we're all pretty much feeling the impact of inflation. The price of gas at the pump most of us are paying close to five dollars a gallon and we all know that what you're getting at the grocery store is just not the same dollar value from before. For example looking at groceries, a basket of groceries that cost a hundred dollars in 2021, just last year, is now going to cost you 108 dollars in 60 cents based on that 8.6% inflation figure. Normally when we have that target inflation of roughly 2%, we're not really feeling inflation that much at the pump or with our housing costs or at the grocery store, but 8.6%, you better bet that we're feeling it. To understand how important it is to understand this right now and be aware of inflation, we have to look back in history and this is literally the highest inflation since 1981. If we go all the way back we had a big spike in the 1980s. That is the last time that inflation has been this high. Right now we're at roughly a 40-year high with our inflation numbers and the way things are going we might just be at a 50-year or 100-year peak, the way it is looking. Hopefully that's not the case. We do have the fed aggressively increasing rates to fight that inflation, but we are still seeing this number creeping up. That's inflation - now onto the investment side. There's some investments out there that are going to get absolutely destroyed in an inflationary environment and a lot of us have experienced that because they are parts of our portfolios, especially young people. Things like speculative growth, cryptocurrencies etc., anything like that is getting absolutely destroyed in this inflationary environment. The question becomes what investments out there ignore inflation entirely and it comes down to two core factors. Number one is inelastic demand and number two is low correlation to the stock market.

Starting off with inelastic demand, this is companies that produce a product or service that people need, regardless of the price. Think about things like toothpaste, toilet paper, your utility bill - this is the things that we pay for no matter what, whether it's a good economy or a bad economy. Prescription, medications etc - things of that category. As far as low correlation to the stock market goes, the CPI or the Consumer Price Index which is the figure that we use to calculate our inflation, this is a measure of all prices for products and services over time. This is one key indicator for the stock market performance, and what has been found is that investments with a low correlation to the stock market typically perform better through inflationary times. There was this hope and pray out there that Bitcoin was this ultimate hedge against inflation but that turned out to be not true. What I did do is I was holding on to gold for a period of time expecting that to have some type of meaningful change because you typically see gold as a good hedge but in this economy we didn't really see that as the case so far with gold prices and so it's important to understand that not every market is going to be the same, in fact it's rarely going to be the same. You are going to have similarities but whatever did well during the last bull market or bear market, or whatever held up during the last inflation cycle, it's probably not going to be the same exact thing this time around.

The first investment with inelastic demand to consider one that I already alluded to is utility stocks. What are utility stocks? These are companies that provide utilities such as water, gas and electricity. One of the advantages is there is a high amount of regulation from the Government. Why utility stocks? Well, demand for utilities is generally inelastic and the Government typically regulates price to maintain specified returns, leading to a very consistent investment and oftentimes you can find higher dividend yields that are relatively consistent. My only cautionary piece of wisdom is that I would not recommend investing in a utility stock that is involved in the supply side of the business, which means they have generation plants and oil or natural gas transmission stations and that is because of this rapidly fluctuating price of commodities. If you have been watching like natural gas prices, I would not personally want to invest in a utility stock that had exposure to the fluctuating commodity prices.

The next investment on the list is commodity stocks or ETFs or Index Funds. What are these exactly? Well commodities include buying and selling as well as trading primary products or raw materials. Examples of this include oil, gold, corn, it could also include natural gas. Why do commodities do well during inflation? That's because commodity pricing usually follows inflation. Think about it this way. Inflation is the increase of the prices of things over time, but if you can gain exposure to the very things that are increasing in price, i.e food or gas you could benefit yourself from those increases. Most people would do this through futures exposure but that's not really the common man's investment that's more so left for the professionals, but there are some investments that could accomplish this for you. More information here on commodities; we have what's called soft commodities and then hard commodities. Soft commodities include agriculture and livestock, things like corn, soybeans, coffee and pork and hard commodities include natural resources, things like gold, oil and rubber. As mentioned you do have some different purchase options. You could use these spot markets for immediate delivery but that's really not going to make sense unless you're looking to take delivery of the underlying commodity. You of course have derivatives which includes futures, forwards and options, but as mentioned 99% of average investors - maybe even 100% should just completely stay out of that space - it is not a scenario where when your average retail investor enters the futures market, they're typically not going to have a good experience, unless you have a lot of prior knowledge about financial markets, and you have all of the expensive software and subscriptions to be on level footing with the professional Wall Street traders. Here's an example of a common man's investment to where you could derive exposure to commodities and this is the SPDR S&P oil and gas Exploration and Production ETF, trading under XOP. Over the last year with this increase in oil prices, this ETF has done very well. To date, they had $4.85 billion in assets under management and an expense ratio sitting at 0.35%, so if you expect the price at the pump to increase which I personally do just to be completely upfront with you, this could be a way to gain exposure, but do bear in mind that you're buying into an ETF that's already up 50% in the last year, so truth be told, the right time to have bought oil was probably a year ago when we first started maybe getting this indication that inflation wasn't so transitory. You want to try to be a little bit faster on these moves, otherwise if you're just moving into oil at the same time as everyone else, the opportunity really might not be there anymore.

Now let's cover an agriculture example which still fits within this umbrella of commodities. We have the Invesco DB Agriculture Fund, trading under DBA - that is the stock symbol. To date, they had $2.31 billion in assets under management however the expense ratio is a little bit higher in this fund coming in at 0.85% and over the last year it has not performed as well as oil, but owning commodities

ETFs when commodities are going up is a relatively profitable activity as long as you get in at the right time. Another common question is what about your savings, because if you are good at managing your money, it's important to have a pool of money that's invested, but also a pool of money that's in cash, that way you have money for an emergency fund or different possible things like that. One of the options available is a startup that I personally invested in myself called Yotta. Based on current inflation data which was in may we've seen an overall 1% increase in prices month over month. On a rolling calendar figure that came in at 8.6% which is our ballpark inflation figure that we are now going off of. So if we now look at the average savings rates using Bank rate, as of June 15th 2022, the average savings account earns just 0.07% API. That means that if you have a thousand dollars sitting in there, you're earning a 0.07% return on that one thousand dollars. When we're in a normal economy and inflation's 1 to 2% the deterioration of your buying power isn't really that big of a deal, but when inflation is coming in at 8.6%, well all of the sudden if you net out that small 0.07% APY, you're seeing a net loss on average of 8.53% of buying power annually. Literally putting your money into a traditional financial institution right now, pretty much means it's a guaranteed way to say goodbye to 8.5% of your money in the next 12 months.

That's why Yotta could be an interesting way to hedge against inflation with your savings as this is a prize linked savings account. You do earn a base APY that's going to be better than average and then on top of that, you have the chance to win up to 10 million dollars every single week, even with your deposits fully FDIC insured. Yotta has been an awesome way to incentivize savings and potentially outpace inflation with the combination of both a savings reward, plus the potential to win prizes every single week. You could literally open up the account with ten dollars if you wanted and then you're going to get a hundred bonus tickets where you could win up to 10 million dollars, fully FDIC insured.

Next we have to talk about TIPs and I'm not talking about what you're going to give your barista at Starbucks - I'm talking about a Treasury Inflation Protected Security. These are by no means a guaranteed way to outpace inflation and you're really not going to outpace current inflation rates based on what we are seeing right now, but it is a way to get a decent rate of return on a large amount of money - up to five million dollars per social security number with a guaranteed return backed by the Federal Government. TIPs have been in the range of 1 to 2% and definitely not north of 2, but it's still much better than your average savings account so if you wanted to get more than that 0.07 and you're okay with locking up your money for a period of time, you could look into these TIPs which can be purchased in 100 increments fully backed by the US Government. These TIPs can be issued in terms of 5, 10 or 30 years and you can of course hold them until redemption or you could also sell them early on the secondary market. Why would somebody own TIPs? Well the principle rises with inflation and at maturity, the investor gets adjusted or the original principal, whichever of the two is higher. That being said the interest payments are going to vary as the rate is multiplied by the adjusted principal. Again, you're not going to outpace inflation with these but it might be a better alternative than just having your money sitting there in the Bank account, especially if you're not looking to invest it, but you're also not looking to deploy it into anything in the near future, like for example if you had 25 grand that was being saved for a down payment on a house, that might be an option where TIPs make sense. The other thing that you should check out is called I Bonds but there is a maximum of ten thousand dollars per social security number.

Next up, what about real estate? Believe it or not real estate has proven in the past to be an inflation resistant investment. We're talking about residential or commercial real estate that is used for housing and we're talking about getting a return on your investment from both property appreciation and monthly rent payments. Why is real estate a good investment during inflation? Well inflation reduces the loan to value ratio, because if prices are appreciating, it's de-risking your asset for you. If you started off at a 80% loan to value ratio which is common for a conventional mortgage, let's say the value of your property appreciates, it could bring you down to a 70% or a 60% loan to value, de-risking your loan, giving you more equity and just making it less risky for you to hold on to that asset. Another reason why real estate is a good investment during times of inflation is because you have the potential to increase your rents without an increase in your mortgage payments. But how do you go about investing in real estate? Well there's a couple of different options. You have crowdfunded real estate platforms which is going to give you private real estate exposure and that is probably the preferred method for most people because you don't want to have all of the volatility of the stock market tied in with your real estate. A lot of people have said, hey why can't I just go out and buy a REIT like Realty Income Corp - you certainly could but just understand that you're going to be susceptible to those same ebbs and flows of the stock market and if you're looking to diversify your portfolio, you ideally want things doing different things at different times. For example me right now, my stock market investments have gone down i have a very limited amount in cryptocurrency under $15,000 right now and but my real estate investments have all gone up lately and have still been going up. That's how a diversified portfolio should work is that while some things are going down this other stuff over here is going up but if you own REITs and the stock market, you might have direct correlation there and that's what we've seen in the past.

Then you have direct purchase which is what I do primarily. I'm not involved in crowdfunding anymore. I own a rental property, I have a house as well and I have a land purchase and it's probably something I'm going to be purchasing more of in the future land as well as different single family residences. Probably not so much on the multi-family real estate side, but that's just based on not wanting to be involved in all of the management. But let's cover an example of a REIT. I know that I said it's not the best option based on that volatility but it is the easiest one for people to go out and buy, typically because if you already have a brokerage account, you can easily invest in a REIT. Realty Income Corp is the monthly dividend company and it's interesting because most dividend stocks pay dividends every quarter, but this stock pays them every single month. Realty Income Corp to date had a dividend yield of about 4.6% and this is a real estate company focused on monthly dividends from predictable monthly revenue derived from real estate. That being said at the pandemic crash we went from 80 to literally just over 40 in two months, so you're talking about a 50 haircut in the most popular monthly dividend stock, if not one of the most popular REITs. That did not happen with my private real estate investments because it's not a highly liquid investment and there's not a market setting a price on it thousands of times a minute so just be aware of that when you invest in real estate through REITs through the stock market, you are signing yourself up for tremendous potential volatility.

Next let's talk about the green stuff – Farmland. This is something that a lot of people just have not been interested in or even broadly aware of as an investment. I've been surrounded by Farmland my whole life so for me this wasn't a foreign concept but as I've explored the United States more I have found that not everybody has grown up in such a rural area to where you may have never even driven by a farm in your hometown. This is very important but believe it or not it's also a damn good hedge against inflation. But what exactly does it mean to invest in Farmland? Well this is investing in real estate but not buildings. We're talking about the land itself and you're going to make money from two different avenues. Number one; you lease the land out or you rent it out to a farmer and then during the time that you rent it out to him or her that individual farmer, that land is appreciating in value and it has historically. What they're able to do on that is grow crops or livestock, they're able to make some money and you cover your costs, hopefully associated with ownership of that land with the rents, maybe you have some positive cash flow from the rents too and then years later when you sell that land, you benefit from that asset appreciation.

Why is land a good hedge? That is because of the inelastic demand and the positive correlation to inflation. Also if you think about it this way, when food prices are going up, people are going to try to increase the supply of grain and corn, which is going to require more space to grow crops, not to mention when people hear about the money being made in livestock and different crops, it might lead more people to get into the business of farming, buying up more land. There's a good saying about land and it's that they are not making any more of it. Obviously you can't make more land and so when you have this potential for growing demand with a fixed supply of land, that is where you have this great potential for asset appreciation, not to mention in the last 20 years I've seen a lot of farms turned into multi-family housing or development, so we're literally destroying Farmland - meaning we have increasing demand on a dwindling supply, so I am very bullish on Farmland. As far as how to invest in Farmland, you're going to have multiple different options. There are a couple of Farmland REITs out there including Land and FPI - those are the symbols and then there's a plethora of crowdfunding platforms that allow you to purchase acreage or shares of different Farmland deals. That includes Acretrader, Farm together etc., and then of course you have the option for going out and buying a piece of Farmland yourself and then setting up a lease agreement and renting it out to a farmer or you yourself might want to hold on to that land and derive income from it from growing straw, growing trees, all sorts of different ways to make money from the land as it goes up in value. Just for an example here looking at FPI - Farmland Partners Inc, this is that Farmland REIT, to date, they had a market cap of just shy of 700 million and a dividend yield of 1.72% and this is a REIT that manages and acquires high quality farm land with agricultural development potential. You have the same cons of a REIT with the volatility, but it is going to give you the easiest means of exposure right into Farmland. Also a lot of the platforms have a higher minimum investment - sometimes 10 000 or more whereas a REIT the cost is going to be a single share or with fractional shares - it's just whatever minimum is associated with your brokerage account. That's going to wrap up this chapter and I hope this taught you more about inflation, why it's so important to be aware of it and a couple of different investments that could allow you to protect yourself from this deterioration of buying power and these higher prices that are hurting all of us.

Chapter 3 Cash is King

In this chapter we are going to discuss what I will be doing in this bear market and what I have done to prepare. Is it time to get fearful and say oh the bear market is coming tomorrow? Absolutely not, but we do understand that there are bull markets out there and there are bear markets and at some point we are going to see the bear and we need to be ready for it. The first thing I would recommend doing is very simple and that is to increase your cash reserve or your cash pile and it's an option that a lot of people forget about, especially when they're looking at a roaring bull market as they're putting as much money into the market as possible because they're seeing returns. But once you believe the market is becoming overvalued or once you have good profits on the table, it might be a good idea to start increasing your cash pile. Any good portfolio out there has a certain percentage held in cash and that could be for the purchase if an opportunity comes up and there's a certain stock you want to purchase it's good to have cash and remember too that that is not the same thing as your emergency fund. Your emergency fund should not be anywhere near your stock portfolio. Your emergency fund stays in your checking account or in your savings account - it does not stay in your trading portfolio.

So this is not your emergency fund this is cash sitting on the sidelines ready for a potential opportunity. One of the things I recommend is to take some profits off the table, if you have good profits on certain stocks, and the another thing you might want to do as well it's always an option is to take your investment out. Let's say for example you had invested in a hundred shares of a company at ten dollars a share and this was a ten thousand dollar investment and then let's say you had 100% return on that investment you did really well and so now that is a hundred shares at twenty dollars a share worth twenty thousand. Well if you still want to have some skin in the game but you also want to increase your cash pile, you always have the option of taking your investment out of it. In this scenario you could sell half of it or fifty shares at twenty dollars a share and get that ten thousand dollars back out of it and then leave the other ten thousand in the market and let that money ride, so at that point you're playing with house money so that's always an option you have as well is to take your investment out and let your earnings or your profits ride at that point. But what I did and this was completely unrelated to the market but back in January when I thought I was going to be buying a house I had sold a lot of my stocks. I sold Amazon, I sold Google, I moved a lot out of the markets and increased my cash pile and then when that whole house situation fell through I still had a lot of cash I have to return to the market but I'm going to be keeping a good pile of cash right now at least probably 30% to 50% held in cash just waiting for a good buying opportunity. Cash is king at the end of the day. It's never a bad thing to have cash. You don't want to have too much cash sitting around to the point where it's losing its buying power due to inflation, but it's always good to have some cash on the sidelines, especially if you're expecting there to be a bear market. The other thing that you can do as well when it comes to investing and increasing your cash pile and related to bear market investing is to use a trailing stop order. Let's say you are invested in the market, you have a stock that you've made a decent return on and you're going to sell once it falls but you don't want to sell right away, one thing you might want to do is set up a trailing stop order - it's a type of market order and it's quite common and what that does is you can set it so if you have a certain percentage drop intra-day or in one trading day it's going to automatically sell that stock for you. Let's say for example you wanted to have a trailing stop order set at minus 7% so if at any point in time during one trading day that stock falls more than 7%, you're automatically going to sell and so that's what you're going to do. For example let's say on one trading day the stock climbs 10% the next it falls 5%. Well it didn't fall seven in that trading day so it doesn't execute that sell order. Next day you climb seven, the day after that you climb seven but then the fifth day it falls 10% well as soon as that stock falls 7% in one day it executes a sell order and then you no longer own those shares because you sold them but there is one thing you have to keep in mind when you're using this type of order is that that stock could fall 6% on day one and 6% on day two 6% on day three and your order didn't execute because it's set at minus seven, so you could lose 18% over the course of three days and not have that order executed, just because it didn't fall seven in one trading day so just be careful when you're using those trailing stop orders just because there's always the potential for that stock to fall over a longer span of time than one trading day, so you always want to monitor that as well not just assuming this is going to be protecting you. There's always that downside risk of worrying about that stock falling a little bit each day and not having such a massive movement in one trading day.

In summary, holding cash is a great idea as far as the percentage goes and that comes down to your investing strategy. I'm probably going to be aiming for 30% to 50% cash right now and this just comes from me taking profits off the table once I say okay this company is becoming overvalued or okay I'm happy with this return I'm going to take some profits or maybe I'm recognizing long-term capital gains or whatever the situation is - it's good to have cash - cash is king. The other thing you might want to do is consider taking your money out of it and letting the profits ride and playing on house money or possibly using a trailing stop order.

Chapter 4 Dollar Cost Averaging

Now we're going to be covering the second topic which is very simple it's called dollar cost averaging. This is one of my favorite strategies when it comes to investing whether or not you're in a bull market or a bear market because it keeps you out of trouble. It keeps you out of buying at the top of the market and buying in when stocks are overvalued and what happens is over a long stretch of time you're paying the market average for ownership of this stock. What you're going to find in bull markets stocks become overvalued and then in bear markets stocks become undervalued and somewhere in between you find a fair evaluation of what you should expect to pay for that stock. What happens when you dollar cost average is you're buying shares over a long span of time and so as a result you are paying the market average price for those shares. What you're doing here is investing the same dollar amount every single month and this all comes down to what you can reasonably afford - maybe for somebody it's a hundred dollars a month, maybe it's 500, for me I usually try to put anywhere from one to three thousand a month of new money into the market every single month but it all depends on where you're at financially and how much money you can funnel into the market. What you're doing here is you're slowly accumulating shares over a long span of time and over time you're going to be paying the market average for those shares. What happens normally is people get excited during a bull market and they say okay I'm going to funnel more money into the market they're seeing a return, but as soon as they see a bear market they stop putting money into the market. They become fearful and they say oh I'm losing money in the stock market i better not put any money into it and that is when you run into trouble because you're going to want to be continuing to funnel money into the market in order to be lowering your cost basis or smoothing that number and paying that average price. So make sure that if anything you're putting more money into the market during a bear market and less during a bull market. When it comes to investing the right thing to do often feels like it's wrong emotionally because it's a little scary, but during a bear market that's the time when you want to be funneling more and more money into the market. What you're doing is slowly accumulating shares over a long span of time and as a result paying the market average price per share. You're buying at the same time every single month or maybe you're doing it weekly and you're buying the same amount as it's going down in the same amount as it's going up and as a result you're paying pretty much the market average over that long span of time. Just to use an example here numbers wise let's say you were looking at a stock and you started buying shares at seven dollars a share so you bought ten shares at seven dollars ten shares at six dollars ten shares at five ten at four ten at three. Well your cost basis on those shares is five dollars a share. Despite the fact that that stock you started buying at seven and six dollars a share your average price paid per share is five so you own fifty shares at five dollars a share and that's what you're doing by dollar cost averaging as you're buying shares over a long span of time. You're accumulating them slowly and as a result you are smoothing out the price you're paying and you're making sure you're not buying at the top of the market. Anybody who is just now starting to get into the stock market I would do no lump sum investing at the top of the market at the top of a bull market you're just asking for trouble. Instead follow a dollar cost averaging type strategy and this works with stocks, this works with ETFs - one of my favorite ways to dollar cost average is into dividend stocks. I will buy into dividend stocks or dollar cost average and then I'll also set that up with a drip so my dividends are reinvested and we're going to talk about this later on but one of my favorite things to do during a bear market is to go hunting for dividends and invest in dividend stocks. Dollar cost averaging is a great strategy for dividend investing because you're making sure you're paying the market average or the fair price for those shares and you're also reinvesting those dividends with a drip, so my number one strategy when it comes to bear markets is dollar cost averaging. I hope you can see why that is and that is my favorite strategy to follow and the one I recommend to beginners, especially if you're just now getting into the market - dollar cost average.

Chapter 5 Bear Market Strategy - Dividends

In this chapter we're going to move on and talk about my third bear market investing strategy which is dividends - it's to go hunting for dividends. One of the easiest things you can do during a bear market is look for stocks that have a strong dividend history they have been paying dividends for a long time and rising those dividends and look for high dividend yield stocks. You're not going to go out there and sort by the highest dividend yield and start buying stocks with a 20% dividend just because high dividends are often a trap, but what you can do is you can calculate that dividend coverage ratio to make sure this company can afford to pay that dividend and if this is a company with a high dividend that has the ability to pay that dividend based on the coverage ratio and they've been growing dividends for a long time and they have a long history of paying dividends, that would be a great time to pick up shares of that stock and take advantage of that dividend. This is fundamental stock analysis 101. To calculate the dividend coverage ratio, all you're going to do is take the annual earnings per share and the best way to do this is to use the 12 trailing months of data and then divide out the annual dividends paid per share and that essentially tells you how much the company is passing along to shareholders and dividends relative to their earnings. What number are you looking for? Below one is bad - that means that companies paying more in dividends than they're earning and as we know dividends are not guaranteed and they can be cut really at any point in time and so if you're investing in a company that's paying a higher dividend than they can even afford they're paying more in dividends than they're earning, then there is a strong potential for a dividend cut. One to one point five I'm calling that "meh" it's not very good either because that means that company is paying a lot in dividends and they're likely going to be restructuring that in the future whether that means a cut or they are going to be cancelling that dividend altogether. What I'm looking for is a dividend coverage ratio of a 1.5 to 3 and that's going to be a good healthy dividend coverage ratio and that means that company can afford to pay that dividend. On the other side of the coin here when that dividend coverage ratio climbs above three, and it's a three plus that means that company might be greedy and they are retaining too much of their earnings for themselves and not passing along the dividends or the earnings to shareholders in the form of dividends. You want to look for a happy medium there of a 1.5 to 3 and that generally means that company can afford to pay that dividend. What else can you look for as far as dividends? Like we said you want to look at the dividend history as well as the growth streak and there's no real resource to find this - you just have to research it on your own or look at the dividend history and see if they've ever had a period of time where the dividend was flat or decreased, because the thing is that companies are going to want to increase their dividends. They want to have a strong growth streak because that's going to attract investors. Most companies at all costs the worst thing they can do is cut their dividend and they're only going to do it if it's absolutely necessary because they know as soon as they cut that dividend the share price is going to fall as a result. They want to keep shareholders happy, they want to keep that dividend growth streak up and so a dividend of a company that has been paying dividends for decades and they have a decade-long growth streak, that's a pretty safe dividend. They're only going to cut those if it's an absolute necessity and one example of this is Pfizer - that was a company that had to cut their dividend in 2008 and 2009 but they had a very long growth streak but because it was the depths of a recession they absolutely had to cut that dividend, but most companies are going to try to cut everywhere else other than that dividend just because they don't want to piss off the shareholders. The other thing that you have to realize is that during a true bear market in the depths of a bear market, it's possible to find a stock that's been battered and dragged down by the overall market with a 10% dividend yield that's a sound investment, and just the idea behind a 10% yield is crazy because that means that if you bought that stock and even if the stock did nothing, well in 10 years you got your money back just in those dividends, and so it's not out of the realm of possibility to find a stock with a 10% dividend yield during a bear market. So one of my favorite strategies when investing in a bear is to go out there and start hunting for these dividends and check the coverage ratio, check the dividend history and make sure they have a history of paying this dividend and then scoop up the shares of some dividend stocks out there of companies that you like and then reinvest those dividends and accumulate some serious wealth in the process. The best thing you should do here is obviously like we said earlier dollar cost average that's one of the best strategies for a bear market is accumulate shares over a long span of time, and also set up a drip a dividend reinvestment plan or program, that way all of your dividends are being reinvested back into the issuing stock and as I'm sure you know that this allows your dividends to earn more dividends and in the process you earn that compound interest and that is something that will make you very wealthy just in and of itself. The final thing I'm going to say as far as dividends go, don't be dazzled by dividends. So many people are dazzled by dividends they go out there and they see a 20$ dividend yield and they go oh my gosh I can get my money back in five years this is amazing but they don't realize that the reason that dividend yield is so high is because that stock has fallen massively in the short term and likely a dividend cut is around the corner. So always start off by looking at the stock, look at the actual company check out the balance sheet make sure they have sound operations, look at the dividend history, the growth streak and the coverage ratio and if all of that checks out then it's probably a good stock to consider investing in for dividends but don't solely rely on the dividend yield.

Chapter 6 How to Find Value

Now we're moving on to my other favorite investing strategies when it comes to bear markets and that is just simply finding the value - it's all about applying those principles we learned taking a deep dive with these companies looking at the financial documents looking at the balance sheet and determining whether or not this is a financially stable or financially healthy company, and then look for a company that is trading at a price that is below the underlying value. That's all about what Benjamin Graham talks about and Warren Buffett is that you're going to want to be greedy when others are fearful and the thing about a bear market is there's widespread fear everywhere, people are afraid of stocks, they want to do anything they can to get them off their hands and so as a result that price starts to fall and fall and it gets to a point where that price is well below the underlying value of that ownership right of that company. But how do you find the value? Well, these are a few of the things that I would look for if it is a bear market and I'm ready to invest in some good durable companies that are being battered by the market. First of all one of the most important things to look for is low debt load this company has. Look at both the short-term debt and the long-term debt and make sure this company is not burdened with debt. I always like investing in companies with a low debt load. A good example of this is Google or Facebook companies without a lot of debt because they have more of the ability to weather a storm and I always compare the balance sheet of a company to like my own balance sheet and about if I was this company and if I had a lot of debt and I had to pay back that debt and all of a sudden I was making less money I'd be in a pinch, but if you look at a company with very low debt and even if they are starting to see less revenue, well they don't have as much debt they're not paying as much interest on that debt so they can weather that storm a little bit better and so that's always what about that is why I look for companies that have a low debt load. That's what I look for you can see that on the balance sheet looking at the current assets current liabilities and also look at the liquidity ratios for a company and then the other thing to consider here is the operating history. Are we looking at a blue chip stock that's been around for a hundred plus years or are we looking at a stock that's been around for five ten years - what are we looking at here, because you have to realize that companies that have been through these storms before going to have better success and they're more durable and time-tested. Look at a stock like 3M or General Mills - they've been through so many bear markets they're going to be able to weather that storm better than a stock that's brand new so you always want to think about that and 3M and General Mills are more defensive investments but even a stock like Apple that's been around for a long time they've been through bear markets where they're going to see periods of less discretionary spending on their products but they're able to weather that storm because they've been through it already. That's something I always consider as well is this a company that's been around for a long time or is this a brand new company that has never been through a bear market before and I always like to invest in those companies that have been through it before and they are time tested. As far as looking for the debt load of a company one of the best things you can do is just look at the current ratio - it's one of the liquidity ratios and I would brush up on all those and become familiar with those. The current ratio is very simple to calculate. You take the current assets on the balance sheet, divided by the current liabilities and that's going to give you an idea of the asset to liability ratio as far as short-term assets and short-term debt and you want to find a company with a 1.5 or above. The higher that number is the better off but if the current ratio is below one - that means that the company has more current liabilities than they do have current assets and that would be something you are not looking to see. Past that looking at the current ratio looking at the liquidity ratios - what you can look for in a late bear market when it's going to start to hopefully emerge into a bull market you're going to want to start looking for growth and you can look for growth in two places. First of all you can look for top line growth in terms of revenue growing or second of all you can look for bottom line growth in terms of earnings growing, but that's usually one of the first indicators that a company is going to be turning around is when you start to see top line growth for that company and you start to see revenue numbers turning around and starting to increase. Then other things you can look for look for companies that are restructuring, look for companies that are having layoffs, look for companies that are having consolidation. Now you do have to be careful here because you don't want to be investing in companies that are shutting down and really winding down their operations, but if you're looking at a company that's been around for a long time, a blue chip stock and you hear about them having layoffs and cutting back and reducing their expenses and their operations, that's usually a good sign as far as that consolidation and restructuring goes. If you're looking at a brand new company and you hear that they're laying off 50% of their staff, that wouldn't be a good sign obviously but looking at a time-tested large company having some layoffs and some consolidation, I do see that as a good sign but I know a lot of people would disagree with me on that one, but that is something that I look for and it's something I saw going on with General Electric when I was looking at that stock when you heard about them doing layoffs and consolidating I see that as a positive for a stock like that. Other than that other fundamental indicators to look for is look for a peg below one that means that that stock is undervalued based on their anticipated growth potential. In general looking for a low price to earnings or a low forward PE based on the industry and then also take a look at that PB ratio because if that stock is trading at a price to book below one that means that stock is trading below the actual book value for those shares. But the other final piece of advice I'm going to have for you in a bear market just keep it simple. Bear markets are not the time for complicated investing strategies really there's never a time for that in my opinion, but if there was ever a time to do it it's not during a bear market. During a bear market keep it simple. Look for durable companies blue chip companies that are being battered by the market, look for strong dividends and a strong dividend history, analyze the fundamentals and find the value and start scooping up shares of undervalued companies and that's pretty much as simple as it gets and don't be too complicated with your strategy. It's certainly not the time to be playing around with things you're not experienced with just in my opinion but of course that is up to you and it's going to be a learning experience if you're wrong about it or if you're right, maybe it will pay off.

Chapter 7 Bear Market Strategy: Short Selling

In this chapter we're going to be talking about another bear market investing strategy and this is one that I don't do myself but a lot of people do this and this is a strategy known as short selling. There's a number of different reasons why I am not somebody who short sells and one of them we're going to discuss when I go over an example of what can happen when you're short selling and you're wrong about your particular bet, you can lose a massive amount of money when it comes to short selling. There are a number of different reasons why I personally do not recommend it but I just wanted to expose this idea to you in case you are interested in doing more research on your own and learning more about this investing strategy, but just understand that I personally do not get involved with short selling and I don't necessarily recommend it, especially for beginners but if you're a seasoned investor and what you're doing and you have a massive amount of risk tolerance, then maybe short selling is something that makes sense to you. In order to identify what short selling is we have to start by talking about the opposite, which is what most of us are familiar with, it's the type of investing that I do and it's called long investing.

Long investing is very simply betting that a particular stock or asset is going to go up in value. So maybe you liked Microsoft stock for example, if you were long on Microsoft that would mean you're betting that stock is going to go up in value so you make money by buying shares of that stock and then down the road selling them at a higher price. A short seller is looking to do the exact opposite. They're looking to make money when the stock goes down in value and so when you're short selling you're betting that the stock will go down in value. This is a very complicated process here a lot of people don't understand how this really works how can you make money when a stock price falls, but essentially what you're doing is you're borrowing shares of that stock from your broker, you borrow shares you're going to sell them to somebody else and then down the road at some point in time you have to buy back the same number of shares from the market and return those to your broker and in that meantime there while you are borrowing those shares you're paying interest to your stock broker, so it's a lot more confusing than a bullish investing strategy where you're just buying shares and selling them down the road. When you are short selling there are a number of different factors involved. One of those being margin interest paid to your broker for the duration of time that you are borrowing those shares that you are short selling.

The other thing you have to know about short selling is that you can't do this in a traditional brokerage account and most people out there are in what's called a cash account. I have a cash account and that is what I use. With a cash account all of your securities are paid in full at the time of purchasing or within three days when those funds are settled or those the actual trade is settled so your shares are paid for in full and you are not borrowing money to pay for your shares. So if you're looking to buy 10 shares of Microsoft stock, you would need to have enough cash in your brokerage account to pay for those shares immediately. That's what you have to do with a cash account. On top of that there is no borrowing of any kind, you are not borrowing money from your broker and you're not borrowing shares like with a short sale. There's no short selling, there's no day trading there are pattern day trader rules that you have to follow if you are doing any short term or swing trading. During a trading week you have to be familiar with those or you can get in trouble. There are day trading requirements pattern day trader rules you have to have a certain amount of money or a certain amount of value in your account at all times and so there's all that involved as well. But the most important part for me is that with traditional investing with in a cash account your maximum loss potential is one hundred percent.

Worst case scenario you invest in a stock and that company goes Bankrupt and you never get any of that money back - that's the most you can lose is 100% of your investment in a cash account.

Now on the other hand let's talk about a margin account. A margin account is what you have if you are a day trader or if you are looking to short sell stocks. This is going to happen in a margin account because you have to borrow those shares from your broker and there is no borrowing in a cash account. With a margin account essentially what happens here is if you are looking to buy stocks on margin and margin is just giving you leverage you're borrowing money to buy stocks, they will usually loan you one dollar per one dollar you have in your account or invested in other stocks. So if you have ten thousand dollars in your brokerage account, your broker will lend you typically another ten thousand dollars you can use to invest in stocks and then you're investing with margin and your idea is that by investing that ten thousand dollars you're borrowing from your broker, you're going to be able to get a better return than you're paying an interest. Some people want to have leverage and they want to have additional money to invest that they don't have so they borrow it from their broker. With a margin account there is usually a credit check involved because they are loaning you money they're going to be running your credit, whereas with a cash account they just need to verify your identity, so it's a little bit more difficult to open a margin account and margin interest is paid to your broker, typically this is paid monthly, or there are services like Robinhood has Robinhood Gold and you pay a dollar amount monthly fee to have a certain amount of buying power available to you, but you have to understand that with a margin account your stocks in your account are your collateral for that debt and so this is something called a margin call, where if you make a bet on a particular stock if you're doing a short sale or if you're using margin and all of a sudden you fall below that margin requirement, you're going to get a call from your broker or notification saying hey you need to deposit more money into your account, otherwise we're going to sell some of your stocks for collateral because we don't believe you have the ability to pay us back for this loan that we gave you. That's something you have to watch out for in a margin account is a margin call and with a margin account you have above a 100% loss with that investment. Let me go ahead and go over an example of that for you now just so this is easy to understand of a short sale that goes wrong. Let's say you're looking to short 100 shares of a stock at 100 per share. So you borrow those shares from your broker you sell them to somebody else for a hundred dollars a share and so you have this short position at $100 per share 100 shares so it's a $10,000 short on this particular company. You're paying margin interest for a period of six months and you're paying 6% interest so in those six months you pay three hundred dollars of margin interest to your broker. Down the road you cover this position - you were wrong about your short sale and you cover at $250 per share so the stock was 100 a share you thought it was going to go to 10 but instead it went to 250. It went completely in the wrong direction. You cover at 250 per share which means you have to go buy a hundred shares off the market at $250 for $25,000. So how much did you lose on this short sale? Well you lost $25,000 in the means of having to buy that off the street or buy that off the market to give that back to your broker and you also lost three hundred dollars of the margin interest that you paid in that period of time, so on that investment there on that ten thousand dollar short sale you lost $25,300. That is what is dangerous about short selling - that is something that a lot of people don't understand is that you can lose a lot more than 100% of your investment and so that right there is a big reason why I don't get involved with short selling, is that the losses are potentially infinite. But if you are interested in short selling I'm definitely not going to be the one to educate you on this just because I've never done it myself and I never will be doing it. I'm also not somebody who gets involved with options and I know a lot of people will use options for bear market investing strategies, but again it's not something I do myself so I don't educate people on things I'm not doing but that is something you might want to explore and learn more about yourself but I'm definitely not an expert on it and I just wanted to explain to you why I don't short sell. It's because of this reason right here.

Chapter 8 Bear Market Strategy: Inverse ETF

In this chapter we're going to be talking about a financial instrument called an Inverse ETF and this is very similar to short selling what we covered in the last chapter. This this is not something I do on my own. I do not invest in Inverse ETFs or leveraged ETFs. I just want to expose this to you just so you are aware that these financial instruments exist and if you want to do further research on your part and invest in these that is completely up to you, but understand that I am not investing in Inverse ETFs and I don't recommend it. I am a bullish investor and I believe there are opportunities to make money in a bullish manner in both bull markets and bear markets and so I would much rather prefer to buy shares of an undervalued stock in a bear market or invest in dividend stocks than I would invest in something like an Inverse ETF. They're very complicated financial instruments and I don't have enough risk tolerance for this type of investment. It's just not for me. The amount of risk involved is just something that I'm not comfortable with. But I'm going to tell you a little bit more about them just so you can have a basic understanding of what Inverse ETFs are. Inverse ETFs are a collection of derivatives and a derivative is simply something that derives its value from something else entirely. It's a collection of derivatives with the goal of profiting from the decline in the value of an underlying benchmark. To explain that very simply it goes in the opposite direction of that benchmark in a one-to-one ratio, if it's an Inverse ETF with no leverage involved. A couple of examples here; PSQ is an Inverse ETF that does the exact opposite of the Nasdaq, so if the Nasdaq goes up 1%, this ETF is going to go down 1% or very close to 1%. It's not guaranteed but they try to do this as closely as possible. DOG is the Inverse of the Dow Jones Industrial average and it's going to do the exact opposite within one trading day and then SH is the Inverse ETF for the S&P 500 and it's going to do the opposite of that, so if the S&P 500 goes up 2% this will go down very close to 2% in that day.

Beyond that we have something called a leveraged ETF. A leveraged ETF amplifies the returns of the underlying benchmark typically in a two to one or three to one manner. It's very similar to margin where you're borrowing money to increase your buying power but you're not paying margin interest in this case with a leveraged ETF. A leveraged ETF is going to amplify the return of that underlying benchmark whether it's a bull ETF or an Inverse ETF. An Inverse leveraged ETF is going to amplify the profit or loss from the change in the underlying benchmark and if you are getting confused by this, it just goes to show you this is a very complicated financial instrument, it is not for beginners and it's not something that I invest in myself it's very complicated but if this is something that's making sense to you maybe you're going to explore this on your own. But just a couple of examples here QID is a leveraged Inverse ETF of the Nasdaq so it's going to do the exact opposite of what the Nasdaq does in a two to one manner. If the Nasdaq were to go down 1%, this fund would go up 2% or very close to 2% and if the Nasdaq went up 2%, this fund would go down roughly 4%, so it does the exact opposite of what the Nasdaq does, but with a two to one ratio of leverage. DXD is the negative 2x of the Dow Jones Industrial average and SDS is the negative 2x of the S&P 500.

Beyond that we have another type of Inverse ETF or leveraged ETF available that is going to be sector specific and these are going to be doing the same thing but the underlying benchmark is an actual sector. For example SKF is going to do the exact opposite in a two to one manner of the Dow Jones US Financial Sector or Index and then the SSG is going to do the exact opposite in a two to one manner of the Dow Jones US Semiconductors Index. So for example let's say you were very bearish on the financial sector, you might say I'm going to buy shares of SKF and I'm going to be having a leverage to bet against the Dow Jones financials Index and you're betting against these companies through derivatives. This is the thing here; this is not as risky as short selling because potentially you can lose 100% of your money here if that ETF goes to zero and understand that it's in only in very rare circumstances that Inverse ETF could go to zero. I spent a lot of time researching this I could not find any examples of one that did, but there was a time when a couple of leveraged ETFs in both oil and natural gas were very close to going to zero, but for this to happen it would have to have a massive intraday move in that underlying benchmark. We would have to see oil or natural gas prices fall like 20 or 25% in one trading day for this ETF to go to zero, but it can happen and it is possible for a leveraged or in Inverse ETF to in fact go to zero so it's something you have to keep in mind but it's not as risky as short selling but this is not something that I personally get involved with myself, I just wanted to let that these are out there and you're going to want to do a lot more research on these before you start investing in them because they are very complicated.

Chapter 9 Best Recession Stocks To Buy Before Bear Market

In this chapter we're going to be talking about the best recession-proof stocks. A lot of people out there are talking about the stock market and whether or not we're going to be going into another correction or a stock market crash going into 2022. Hence have put together a list of stocks for you if you are looking to maybe get a list of some safer investments that have panned out relatively well in the recent recessions or stock market crashes that we have had. First we're going to talk about the performance of the S&P 500 during the two most recent recessions or crashes. The COVID recession that we had was one of the fastest in history in terms of the recovery. But rather than just throwing out random names of stocks and saying "Hey these are good ideas during a recession." We're going to be looking at the data and comparing the returns of those investments during the last two recessions to the S&P 500. Because at the end of the day the goal that you should have during a market downturn with a recession-proof stock is that you want that stock to outperform the overall market or the S&P 500. So probably during a recession almost everything is going to go down somewhat for a period of time, but it's a question of whether or not the stocks that you're holding or the funds that you're holding go down equal to the S&P 500 more than the S&P 500 or less than the S&P 500. For a recession-proof stock what you're looking for is more of that downside protection during a market correction which could lead to a market crash. So it's not so much about the upside that these investments have and during times of good bull markets, well there's times when these investments underperformed the market and it's about how these investments respond when the floor gets yanked out from under the stock market. That is what we care more about not so much the performance of these stocks in a multi-year bull market which really had just a very short blip there during that COVID recession. But that being said the data we're going to go off of here is looking at the correction from the 2008 recession. That was a 40.5% drop in the S&P 500 and then during the COVID recession it was a drop of around 25.2%. Since February of 2020 there's been a massive rally with the S&P 500 up over 34% and this along with inflation worries and eventual Fed tapering is what a lot of people are then saying "Hey maybe we're going to be due for another correction or a crash in the future." Also it's important to think about how long these recessions last because the most recent one that we had was really not a real market recession and even somebody like myself has been conscious really of the stock market during a real recession. During the 2008 recession I remember my dad being stressed out but I wasn't an active participant in the market. During that recession it took a year and a half for that recession to finish out and then for us to come out of it. Whereas during the COVID recession it literally only took two months. So just understand that that's not really what normally happens. The most recent recession that we had was not your typical recession. Starting off with number one on the list is none other than Walmart trading under the symbol WMT. If you take a look at the performance of this stock during that COVID recession we really had barely any blip here whatsoever with Walmart stock. During the 2008 recession when we said the market's dropped around 40%, this gained 1.1% which is way outpacing the S&P 500 and during the COVID recession they gained 5.6%. That being said since, February they're only up 17.2 whereas the overall S&P 500 was up somewhere around 35. So there was a lot better downside protection. In fact you made money as a Walmart shareholder during the last two recessions but it is important to note that it did underperform the S&P 500 coming out of that COVID recession. Walmart are founded in 1962. Market cap of $413 billion. They are a dividend aristocrat. They've been increasing dividends every single year for 48 years and they currently have a dividend yield at 1.48%. Now why is Walmart a good recession-proof stock? Well it comes down to the fact that Walmart's unique identifier is known as EDLP or Everyday Low Prices. When discretionary spending is down Walmart revenues go up. Quarter one revenue 2020 was up 8.6%, versus that same quarter in 2019. What it sort of comes down to is this. Some of us have to shop at Walmart because we need to make sure we're getting the most out of every dollar that we have. Nobody goes to Walmart for the shopping experience. It's terrible but we do it because it's cheap and at times when money is tight or we're uncertain about the future, you're going to see a lot more people going to a Walmart than you would maybe going to a Whole Foods, especially if you're tight on money. So it's a necessary evil in a lot of ways that a lot of people have to save money and shop at Walmart or maybe you're a savvy shopper and you don't really care about the stores being crowded or long checkout lines and maybe you do online ordering or something. But Walmart has done well in the last two recessions. That is why they are number one on the list here for recession-resistant or recession-proof stocks.

Coming in at number two is a name that I don't ever really talked about and in terms of comparing this company to the size of Walmart this is less than

1/10 of the size of Walmart so this is a mid-cap company, not a large or a mega cap but still a pretty large company that's been around all the way since 1928. That is General Mills trading under the symbol GIS headquartered in Minnesota with a current dividend yield of 3.2%. We want to compare this as to how it performed during the '08 recession and then the COVID recession. During the '08 recession we saw that the stock went up 2.3% and during the COVID recession this stock went up 9.3%. However as was to be expected with these stocks, it has underperformed the S&P 500 coming out of that recession. You can't really have the goal of outperforming the market and having downside protection. It's like wanting to have your cake and eat it too. At a certain point you do have to pick one or the other. Am I looking for beating the S&P 500 and a bull market or am I looking for downside protection in a bear? Very rarely you are going to find a stock that's going to offer you both. But why is General Mills a good recession pick? During recessionary times people look towards purchasing more groceries versus eating out. It's a very simple concept. When you have extra money you spend money on entertainment on drinking you go out on date nights and stuff like that and then when you have less money coming in you're going to spend more money on your groceries and probably the more common example these days is Grubhub or meal delivery versus groceries. A lot of people can't necessarily spend all the money they worked for ordering food to their door. So instead they might be doing a shipped order and a grocery order and ordering a bunch of grocery products. General Mills makes a lot of cereals and grains and crackers and things like that so that is why they do well during a recession. And we can see this very clearly because revenue for them in quarter one of 2020 was up 9% versus the same quarter for the previous year. The only difference was in quarter one people weren't going to restaurants. People were buying more groceries. So that is why they are number two on the list.

Number three is a stock I've never owned myself but I have owned Lowe's in the past and did really well. Honestly Home Depot and Lowe's were two of the biggest winners coming out of the COVID recession. Really unbelievable performance here but the downside protection wasn't there as much with these stocks initially. It didn't fall as much as the overall S&P 500 but it did have a negative return during that period. This is another mega cap or large cap company sitting at $428 billion founded in 1978, headquartered in Georgia with a current dividend yield of 1.61% and during the '08 recession this stock had a positive return of 2.4%. During the COVID recession, it did drop 17.7. But what I want to call your attention to is the performance since February of 2020. As we said the S&P 500 returned somewhere over 30%. This is more than double the return of the S&P 500 for that period of time coming out of the COVID recession. So the performance was really stellar here. This might've been a bit unique because of the great reshuffling or the great migration whatever you want to call it where everybody and including myself a lot of people were relocating and then getting involved in home improvement projects because obviously hardware stores were one of the only essential businesses but this is a solid pick during a recession honestly going forward and there's many reasons behind this. One of the main reasons is because during a recession people are less likely to contract work out and the other thing is too you may find that people are staying in their older homes for longer versus selling their house and buying a new apartment. People tend to stay where they're at during a time of uncertainty. And if they're in an older home well as a homeowner or if you don't know there are going to be constant repairs and random stuff you have to fix. What this is saying here is you're more likely to fix those things yourself and be more of a DIY handyman and so that's why Home Depot just tends to do well because whether it's buying things for your projects that are more discretionary where you have a choice around spending it or it's hey I have to fix the siding on my house that's falling off they tend to benefit from both categories. So they are number three on the list and we saw that in quarter one of 2020 when the global markets were collapsing and things were just not looking great for a lot of companies, they grew revenue - was up 7% versus the same period in the previous year.

Number four on the list here is a very boring company probably one that many of us just have not heard of and this company went public in April of 2008 so we can't compare it for the period of the '08 recession. During the COVID recession however when global markets sold off massively this only went down 2.2% which is pretty incredible and since February of 2020 it's up around 26.8%. So it has slightly underperformed the rally of the S&P 500 out of that recession. This is the American Water Works Company Inc. It does definitely deserve to be here on this list. Trading under the symbol AWK. Market cap of $30.9 billion making this a mid-cap stock but this is an old time-tested investment founded back in 1886 headquartered in New Jersey with a current dividend yield of 1.41%. But why is this a good pick during a recession or a time of uncertainty? Well, demand for utilities such as water for example is relatively inelastic so it doesn't really go up and down and change. What we saw here too is and this was probably a result of the stay at home trend with people being at home; you're going to cook more at home, you're going to be running your dishwasher more or just consuming more drinking water at your house versus the office, revenues were up by 3.8% throughout COVID in quarter one of 2020. Water is an essential resource similar to electricity and these are things that no matter what we're just going to pay these bills because we need to have water and we need to have electricity for civilized life. Typically speaking during a bull market it doesn't mean you're necessarily going to be consuming triple the water. You typically just use the same amount of water and just continue about your daily life without thinking about it. As far as cutting back spending you don't really hear a lot of people talking about cutting back on their water usage or consumption maybe during a drought maybe if you're in really dire straits you put a timer in your shower and you take a five-minute shower but it's just not very common. Most people don't think about it. They don't really try to curb their water consumption during a recession. That's usually more for environmental reasons so that's why this is another solid pick on the list here of boring but stable investment during a time of uncertainty.

Coming in at number five on the list is a grocery store giant known as Kroger and this is a company that's another mid-cap stock here with a market cap of $32.5 billion. Very old company founded back in 1883 with a current dividend yield of 1.92%. What was the performance of this stock like in the last two recessions? Well during the '08 recession it did drop 20.5% which was less than the overall S&P 500. However during the most recent COVID recession this stock was a tremendous winner and it was up 14.2%, while the rest of the S&P 500 dipped around 25, and then even coming out of this COVID recession performance has been stellar as well, since February of 2020 up about 56%, so overall Kroger has been a really solid pick in the last two years. It did pretty decent in the '08 recession in terms of outperforming the S&P 500 and it should definitely be on your watch list or your shortlist for recession-proof stocks. Why is this a solid choice here? Though it's not as cheap as Walmart, demand for groceries again increases during a recession for the same reasons as Walmart. Walmart is going to have probably more demand because it's the cheapest option out there. But Kroger again is going to benefit from people doing less dining out people doing less take out and just cooking more meals at home. We saw that in quarter one of 2020 whereas the revenues were up 11.5%.

Coming in at number six on the list is a stock that I've just looked at this stock so many times dating back to even 2017. Obviously at any point in time really if you jumped in on Costco if you held it for the long run you would have done exceptionally well with this stock. Costco has a market cap of $232 billion, founded in 1983, headquartered in Washington and they pay a small nominal dividend here of 0.6%. During the '08 recession they sold off quite a bit. They dipped almost 35%. But the business model for Costco has largely changed since 2008. They are much bigger and better company than they were back then and during the COVID recession they gained 1.4% and they may also be the top performer coming out of the recession on this list with a return of 68.8% since February of 2020. There was really no blip at all. You wouldn't even know there was a recession looking at this stock. So why does Costco do well during a recessionary time? Well even with a membership buying in bulk can provide significant savings and also because people are forced to have a membership with Costco in order to shop with them, it sort of makes you a more loyal shopper to Costco overall because if you're paying for a membership every year or every single month, you're going to want to get the best bang for your buck which means you're probably going to be a relatively exclusive shopper to Costco for those reasons. We've also seen their private brand Kirkland that has beaten many like name brands in terms of sales so they've done really well at selling their own branded products as well so Costco honestly has done exceptional and it will most likely do well in a future recession as well for those reasons. Revenues were up 7.2% in quarter three of 2020, so they also performed well during that recessionary period or coming out of the COVID recession.

Number seven on the list is a company called Waste Management, trading under the symbol WM. Now I will say this I would be a little bit hesitant with Waste Management but I did feel like it should be included on the list because it's another utility stock that tends to have relatively steady demand for the service. Waste Management is obviously a trash and recycling collection company. That I lump in with utilities - these things that you pay no matter what. When people are cutting costs I don't really ever hear of anybody saying "Hey I canceled my trash and recycling pickup and I'm going to Burry my garbage in the yard instead." Nobody does that. You just pay for these things no matter what, making the demand for waste management relatively inelastic. The company has a current market cap of 68.5 billion. Founded in 1968 headquartered in Texas and a current dividend yield of 1.41%.

Revenues were flat all throughout COVID which makes sense because you're not going to really see an increase in the demand for these services. It just is steady pretty much all the time. So for that reason it wasn't necessarily the top performer but it was less of a drop than we saw with the overall market in the 2008 recession and in the COVID recession and it pretty much nearly kept pace with the S&P 500 since February of 2020 falling slightly under it with the overall return here of 31.7%. So Waste Management is not by any means at the top of my list for recession-proof or recession-resistant stocks, but I do think it is one that is still worth keeping on your radar. Especially if it does have a nice pullback it could be a decent stock to accumulate shares of during a recessionary time.

Lastly on the list we have Dollar Tree trading under the symbol DLTR. This company has a market cap of $30.6 billion so it's another mid-cap stock founded in 1986. This is not a dividend payer, but the performance of this stock has been decent during the last two recessions. During the 2008 recession this stock was a huge winner and it went up 60.3% and then during the COVID recession this stock only went down 6.2 which is substantially less than the drop that the overall S&P 500 experienced. And then coming out of the COVID recession this stock had a gain of 56.5% which is pretty dang incredible.

Why did they do well during the COVID recession? It's because discount retailers typically see an increase in demand during recessions. Again it ties back to the same idea we were talking about of people have less money to spend and so they're looking to get the best bang for their buck so discount retailers tend to do well in those scenarios. Also Dollar Tree sells a bunch of groceries and food so if we're eating out less at restaurants and cooking more meals at home more people are going to be buying groceries and items et cetera at the Dollar Tree and we saw this in their revenue figures which were up 8.2% in quarter one of 2020.

The last thing I want to cover quick is where to buy these stocks, should you be interested in making an investment in any of these companies. The number one brokerage that I use is of course M1 Finance and if you are looking for a portfolio-based investing platform, M1 Finance is a really solid brokerage to consider and they offer things like portfolio, dynamic rebalancing, dividend reinvestment, automated contributions and awesome features like that which can allow you to pretty much put your wealth on autopilot. It has a 4.6 star rating in the App Store and they also offer investing borrowing which is a low-cost portfolio line of credit. Then they have a debit and credit card as well which can allow you to earn other cash back rewards and even invest some of that cash back that you earn back into your portfolio. The minimum deposit is $1,000 to get a bonus of $30. But if you wanted to transfer a brokerage account and if you had for example a 50K value account, that you transferred in you would get a $500 bonus.

Chapter 10 Michael Burry's Warning for Stock Market Crash

On May 19 2005 Michael Burry bought his first credit default swaps in anticipation of the housing crisis - 60 million of credit default swaps from Deutsche Bank, 10 million each on six different bonds. His prediction; the US mortgage-backed security once a stable respectable investment product had slowly turned into a dangerous and deceptive time bomb - all caused by greed and corruption. In his eyes this bet was no gamble, he did the digging, he read the documents, he knew what the outcome would be. His problem was that it would take the rest of the world another two years to even start looking it took until the 11th of October 2007 for the S&P 500 to top out at 1,576 points. A year and a half later on the 10th of March 2009, the S&P 500 closed at just 676 points a 57 crash. Michael Burry ended up making a personal profit of a hundred million dollars and made his investors over 700 million from this single bet, but in the years leading up to this amazing success, he received constant criticism from the investing world and even his own investors criticism that ultimately led him to close his fund after all had been said and done. But this happened 15 years ago. Well you guessed it - history is currently repeating itself. It was back in February of last year that Michael Burry first warned of high inflation as a consequence of the FED's unprecedented money printing. He was tweeting to prepare for inflation hashtagging doom to repeat and calling out the us Government and the Federal reserve over the trillions of dollars worth of stimulus they'd done, and at this point he was the contrarian. At the time all looked well. The FED was printing money yes but inflation was staying low. at the time the latest published data showed an annual inflation rate of just 1.7% - that's lower than the FED's target but in classic Burry fashion, he was just early. fast forward 12 months and we're now running at a red-hot inflation rate of 8.6% habitually be one to two years early on literally everything and you two can attain broken clock status Burry tweeted a month ago, of course referencing a tweet made by Elon Musk where he labeled Burry as a broken clock. But what's very interesting is that in the past month or so Michael Burry hasn't just been doing victory laps instead he's been tweeting quite extensively explaining why he believes this economic crisis and subsequent market downturn has only just begun. I certainly don't like to be a big doomsday predictor so please don't take this as me fear-mongering, however I do want to at least cover Michael Burry's full rationale to begin to understand what he's thinking, and yes the overarching message is he believes the worst is yet to come. So much so he thinks the S&P 500 could lose another 50% from where it sits today. On May the 3rd Burry tweeted regarding paradigm shifts and speculative peaks the S&P 500 bottomed 13% lower than 2002's bottom in 2009, 17% lower than 1998's lTCM crisis low in 2002 and 10% lower than the 1970s low in 1975. 15% lower than the Covid low is an S&P 500 value of 1862, roughly she'll appear of 16 nominal P of 9 in historic range. I'm not going to lie I'd read that one quite a few times to get that phrasing but what he's noting is the trend we've seen over the past 25 years is the bottom of a current market crash is usually lower than the one that came before it, by about 10 to 15% adding that 15% below the S&P 500 low that we saw in 2020 takes us down to 1,862 points. That's crazy because it shows that Michael Burry is anticipating a peak to trough fall of 61.4% which would bring us back down to the historical normal Schiller P of roughly 16. Essentially from where we are today Michael Burry anticipates a further 50 + % drop-off in the stock market. It's a bold prediction and it's a prediction that was once again met with criticism as over the past few weeks we saw the market bounce six and a half percent but as we've seen even just across the past few days, short-term bounces certainly don't mean we're out of the woods, and Michael Burry commented on this possible scenario. He recently tweeted "dead cat bouncers are the most epic, 12 out of the top 20 Nasdaq one day rallies happened during the 78% drop from the 2000s top. Nine of the top 20% S&P 500 one day rallies happened during the 86% drop from the 1929 top." That's a lot of numbers to wrap your head around but what he's alluding to here is that even during the worst times, the statistics show that it's quite common to see strong short-term recoveries amongst the longer-term downward trend. 12 of the top 20 Nasdaq bounces happened along this slope, nine of the top 20 S&P 500 bounces happened along this slope. On the 5th of May he added "after 2000 the Nasdaq had 16 bear market rallies over 10$ averaging 22.7% before bottoming down 78%. After 1929 the DOW had 10 bear market rallies over 10% averaging 22.8% before bottoming down 89%." So Burry certainly seems confident that we're simply in the early stages of a much bigger problem and to further his point, he also took the time to comment on the comparatively low trading volumes we've seen during the 2022 downturn thus far. He said top to bottom Microsoft traded 5.2 times shares outstanding by 2002, 3.3 times by 2009 and 0.5 times so far. Amazon traded 5.7 times by 2002, 6.6 times by 2009 and 0.9 times so far. JP Morgan traded three times by 2002, 5.9 times by 2009 and about 0.7 times so far, etc... enough takes time" So really when you look at the trading volumes, even though we've seen the market cool down quite a bit in 2022 and everyone seems bearish from what you hear, the selling really hasn't even started. Withdrawals from the market haven't even really started yet. Money is still flowing into the markets so in Burry's eyes we're likely going to see a lot more selling volume coming over the next few years, which would lead to much larger declines in the stock market. It's a scenario that he said he's not looking forward to facing on the 24th of May he tweeted; "as I said about 2008 it's like watching a plane crash, it hurts, it's not fun and I'm not smiling." That's the interesting thing to remember with Michael Burry is he's seen this happen all before; the first time through the dot-com bubble and the second time in 2008. he's seen these repetitive patterns of human behavior time and time again. He's studied the greed and excess of the major booms and busts and that's what gives him such confidence when he talks about these issues and when he tweets about them. He recently posted a chart to his Twitter which I thought was quite eye-opening.

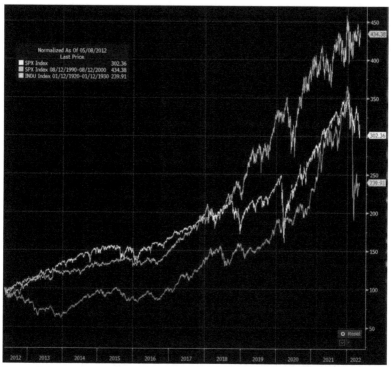

In white we see the 10-year S&P 500 run-up to today. In the yellow we see the run-up to the dot-com bubble and in green the run-up before the great depression. It's pretty scary how similar they are and Michael Burry comments on this saying "third time's a charm, got to love human nature, nothing if not consistent." For him he's seen this pattern of human behavior many times before and he understands where it leads. It was only 12 months back that he was tweeting that he saw the greatest speculative bubble of all time in all things by two orders of magnitude. Perhaps now in his eyes it's been pushed to its breaking point, but of course this is all just the stock market. We have to remember the core reasoning behind Burry's point of view is the economy. We already know Burry's thoughts on inflation and yes we are seeing the FED raise interest rates to make borrowing harder for businesses but we have to remember that interest rate rises also affect the fundamental building block of the economy; the consumer. In harsh inflationary environments that bring about large interest rate rises, unfortunately consumers have less money to spend because more of their savings and income go to servicing their debts. This very frequently starts a negative spiral because less discretionary spending means less sales for the companies that we're invested in. Ideally you want the consumer to be breaking it in, however recently Burry's been hinting that consumers aren't doing too well right now; "US personal savings fell to 2013 levels - the savings rate to 2008 levels, while revolving credit card debt grew at a record-setting pace back to pre-Covid peak, despite all those trillions of cash dropped in their laps. Looming a consumer recession and more earnings trouble." So Burry is quite clearly worried about the depletion of savings, not just because it's pushing everyday people to use more credit cards in an environment of rising interest rates, but also because lowering of savings equals less spending, which hosts the bottom line of these businesses that we're invested in. One anecdotal piece of evidence that Burry referred to recently was Amazon's Q1 results. As CNBC wrote "revenue at Amazon increased 7% during the first quarter compared with 44% expansion in the year ago period. It marks the slowest rate for any quarter since the dot-com bust in 2001 and the second straight period of single-digit growth." Burry responded by saying "and so Amazon says to GDP - there's your weakening consumer" and to follow on from that point, Burry also posted this tweet comparing the US personal savings with GDP.

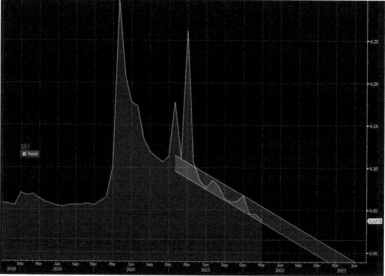

As you can see the savings are covering less and less of America's GDP at a point where America's GDP is shrinking. So overall in Burry's eyes we have inflation, interest rate hikes, reduction in consumer savings, thus less discretionary spending, which ultimately leads to lower profitability of businesses and what we've seen thus far, re-ratings on their stock. In Burry's view we are only in the first inning. It's a very interesting topic to explore and I'm certainly not going to put my hand up and say that I'm the guy that knows exactly which way we're headed next, but Michael Burry is certainly extremely bearish but he quite commonly is.

Chapter 11 Michael Burry's Warning For Recession

It's no secret that in 2022 the stock market hasn't been a particularly nice place to be. The S&P 500 is down about 20% and the NASDAQ is down 27% and from everything we've seen in the news lately it doesn't look like it's getting much better anytime soon. Just last week we got an update that the annual inflation rate in the US has now hit 9.1% with a month-over-month rise of 1.3%. Remember the FED aims for the annual inflation rate to be 2% per year so we've got about eight months worth of inflation in just 30 days. If you delve into the numbers a huge chunk of that inflation is due to the energy crisis we're currently going through thanks to Russia's invasion of Ukraine and also the world's subsequent management of that situation. Energy was by far the worst category in tune up 7.5% month over month and broken down further we can see energy Commodities up 10.4%, gasoline up 11.2% and utility gas or piped gas up 8.2%, so big increases and unsurprisingly the results of this accelerating inflation are big interest rate hikes. The FED is really gearing up now and their next meeting is scheduled for the 26th and 27th of July and economists are expecting at least another 0.75% rise in the Federal funds rate with some even tipping a whole percentage Point rise. The unfortunate reality of the situation is that these interest rate Rises will keep happening until that inflation rate is back down to the FED's Target of 2% annually, so there still could be a lot more to come. But of course what these rate risers mean in reality is that economic conditions continue to get more and more difficult for Citizens and businesses. Consumers have less disposable income as debt payments rise and life's Essentials get more and more expensive and for businesses this means lower profits at a time where their debt repayments and other costs are also rising. For these reasons many are predicting that a nasty recession is just around the corner for America and one person who saw all this coming is the man the myth the legend Michael Burry. But despite predicting all this at the start of last year, he's recently come out suggesting that in his opinion we're only halfway there. But what's the reasoning why he thinks we're only halfway there? He recently tweeted "adjusted for inflation 2022 first half, S&P 500 down 25-26% and NASDAQ down 34-35%, Bitcoin down 64.65%. That was multiple compression, next up earnings compression so maybe halfway there." This is a pretty insane prediction because it means Burry is thinking we're probably going to get down to an S&P 500 value of roughly 2,800 but it's also pretty scary because I agree with his reasoning. But what is he talking about? Well, in that tweet he brings up two factors that contribute to the price of a stock falling; there's multiple compression and then there's earnings compression. Firstly multiple compression; what Burry thinks and we've seen thus far. The most common and simplistic valuation metric that exists is the price to earnings ratio - stock price divided by earnings per share. If your company owns one dollar per share in a year and the stock price is twenty dollars, you have a PE ratio of 20. But we can also rearrange this equation to look like this: stock price equals earnings multiplied by the PE Ratio or in other words the earnings multiple what multiple of earnings are investors willing to pay for the stock. That earnings multiple is very much dependent on what investors think the company is likely to do going forward, so big growth opportunities, great performance ahead, investors will give it a high earnings multiple. Whereas problems with the company, competitions, stealing market share - you'll get a much lower multiple. What it tells you is investor sentiment and what investors are expecting to happen in the future. We can apply this formula to a specific stock but we can also apply it to the market as a whole. The price of the S&P 500 and the earnings on the same chart creates a joy and a Gloom scale. The white air quotes price of the S&P 500 since 1960 and then the blue chart shows the earnings over that same time period.

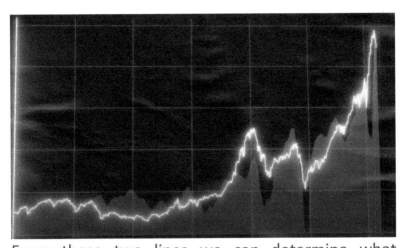

From those two lines we can determine what multiple was put on the S&P 500 during those periods, price over earnings. For analysis sake we're going to show that line compared to the Benchmark of 15.97 which is the average multiple for the S&P 500 over the long term. Sometimes investors are overly optimistic and give the market a higher multiple and then sometimes they're more pessimistic and they give it a lower than average multiple. It goes through Cycles where investors are overly optimistic and then they become pessimistic. Also you might be asking and why there was such optimism in late 2008 that seems a bit weird? Well that's a special case where the earnings were so extremely low during the Great Recession, however at the time prices were being somewhat stabilized because the FED had announced a massive bailout plan, so you get this weird patch at the GFC where prices looked elevated versus earnings, but generally the market goes through patches of optimism and pessimism around the average multiple of 16. Running into 2022 that multiple is falling way back towards the average. In fact this data stops at the start of this year and as earnings have stayed strong so far this year, yet the market has continued to fall, this line is continuing downward through 2022. This is what Michael Burry notes as multiple compression - really it's a fancy way of saying investor confidence is deteriorating. Last year investors were willing to pay upwards of 35 times the earnings of the S&P 500 to own it, now current estimates are that multiple is fall into about 20, so optimism quickly turning to pessimism so the market is falling. That's the main takeaway but it's also affected as well by interest rates, is when interest rates Rise new bonds look more enticing and the big money in the market starts flowing out of the stock market back into the bond market, which drags down the stock market. This is the opposite of what we've been seeing happen over the last few years when interest rates have been very low, and in those times the stock market usually gets artificially inflated because Bond returns are zero, thus the big money looks to put their money elsewhere. But long story short that's multiple compression; Investor confidence weighting and rates Rising. That's the first half of Burry's tweet but as he suggested here's of the opinion that we're only halfway there, and from here he thinks it's earnings compression that takes over so instead of prices being brought down by investor confidence waning, it's also going to be brought down by companies in Corporate America, earning less. Right now because inflation is so crushingly high, interest rates are going up. But in reality what that means is that consumers have less spare cash. What we're seeing right now is people's savings covering less and less of America's GDP at a time where the GDP is going down. Burry tweeted "US personal savings filter 2013 levels the savings rate to 2008 levels while revolving credit card debt grew at a record-setting pace back to pre-covert Peak despite all those trillions of cash dropped in their laps. Looming a consumer recession and more earnings trouble." What he's getting at is unfortunately all this inflation and all these interest rate hikes are leaving consumers with very little in their pocket and less spending also means less revenue for businesses. Couple that with higher costs and increasing costs of debts and all of a sudden you've got corporate earnings really struggling. One company that we saw struggling of Q1 that Burry specifically made an example of was Amazon. If we turn over to Simply Wall Street we can see under the future growth tab that Amazon's earnings were doing all right but they tanked in Q1 - consumers aren't willing to spend as much. Also while I don't put very much weight on analysts expectations, the analysts are expecting that dip to continue through 2023 and start recovering in 2024. So you can see the macro economics in the numbers. Since 2021 the operating expenses have been increasing at a faster than normal rate and the cash flow from operations has reduced. Overall that is the second part of Burry's Tweet. Now that we're seeing significant interest rate hikes and the average consumer is struggling, Burry thinks that from here we're going to start to see the earnings of corporate America falling and remember from our equation, price equals earnings times multiple or investor sentiment. So far earnings have stayed pretty strong but the sentiment has fallen, so now Burry is expecting the macroeconomic environment to start seriously impacting earnings, bringing down the share market even further. Remember that rate hikes won't stop until inflation is backed down where it needs to be and so far we're a long way from that. In fact at the moment we're getting further away each month. So that's what Michael Burry is anticipating over the next little while. Yes, it's a little bit worrying but remember it's nothing to panic about these Cycles are normal and we as investors need to be long-term minded to see them as opportunities. The other thing to remember is that not every company is affected equally. We were just talking about the market as a whole but there are a lot of companies that don't have any debts or their business isn't generally impacted during a recession or they have pricing power so even though they are battling recession conditions, their earnings can still rise. There are these companies that may still shed some market cap with the rest of the market that might be really solid long-term opportunities in these conditions. While recessions suck and we as consumers definitely feel the pinch, remember that you as an investor can still set yourself up to beat inflation and build your wealth. It's not always as Doom and Gloom as the media makes it out to be and really a lot of Fortunes are created in the deepest darkest recessions. Michael Burry the man that famously predicted the 2008 housing bubble is currently predicting another very large recession and stock market crash in 2022 on the back of all the inflation we're currently seeing. In typical Burry fashion he predicted this all the way back in February 2021, so he's always early but at the same time, Burry made another bold prediction - one that completely flew under the radar and that was that cryptocurrencies were in massive bubble territory and were ready to pop. He said "cryptocurrencies are a bubble that pose more risk than opportunity" adding later on that "FOMO parabolas don't resolve sideways when crypto falls from trillions or meme stocks fall from tens of billions, main street losses will approach the size of small countries - history ain't changed" Unfortunately for those heavily in crypto that prediction aged very well. Year to date we've seen Bitcoin fall 57%, Ethereum 70% and even Elon's favorite Dogecoin has fallen 59%. At the start of the year Bitcoin's market cap was 891 billion, currently sits at 369 billion - a 522 billion reduction in approximately six months. It's about the same size as the GDP of Ireland. Burry was right - losses are amounting to the size of small countries but that's not all Burry had to say on crypto. In fact he's been tweeting about it a lot recently as well so in this chapter let's hear what he has to say and what he thinks we as investors should do about it. One thing that should be noted is Burry is not a crypto hater. In fact when it comes to the open ledger system that is the blockchain and the finite nature of many of these coins, he thinks that's pretty smart. He said himself back in 2021 that he doesn't hate Bitcoin and he followed up by saying he believes that most proponents are correct in their arguments for why it's relevant at this point in history. However despite these points there's no doubt Burry has been a critic of Bitcoin over the years for three main reasons. Two have to do with the ideas behind crypto itself, and the other has to do with how investors treat it. Let's run through them and point number one when we're talking about crypto as a currency. Burry has always held the opinion that if it gains too much popularity, Governments will just move to destroy it and this has been a very popular belief of many in the finance sector. He said that in his view the long-term future is tenuous for decentralized crypto in a world of legally violent heartless centralized Governments with lifeblood interests in monopolies on currencies, however in the short run anything is possible and that's why he's not short Bitcoin. While this hasn't been a big contributing factor to the recent crashes we've seen in crypto it is a flaw in the long term thesis of crypto. The reality of this situation is that Governments like to control their currency so if there's anything that could threaten that control of course they will look to crush it and so far we've already seen China outlaw it. But the reason Governments generally haven't crushed it yet, is because at the moment it doesn't pose a very big threat as it's simply used as a financial asset and not really as a currency. However in the long run if Bitcoin or Ethereum did start to gain serious traction and threaten to be an everyday currency that people chose say over the US dollar, the Government would more likely than not use their power to crush it so they can stay in control of their economy. This is a viewpoint that has also been held by macro investing god Ray Dalio. He said: The Governments don't want to have it successful. You have the United States talking about how to regulate it and it could still be controlled. At the end of the day if it's really successful they'll kill it and they'll try to kill that and they will kill it because they have ways of killing it." That's Burry's first point, the Governments will crush it but beyond this one huge argument we've seen from the crypto community over the past years that cryptocurrencies are a great hedge against inflation, because the idea here is that because many of these coins Bitcoin for example only have a finite number that will ever be created then an asset like that should hold up very well against the dollar during inflationary periods like what we're seeing now - periods where the Federal Reserve prints just a ton of money and consumers in the Government do a lot of spending and inflation just skyrockets. People also say this about gold. Gold is a finite resource and therefore generally performs well during periods of economic instability. Unfortunately for crypto currencies like Bitcoin however this hypothesis has just not worked out in reality, proving that at least at this moment in time Bitcoin is seen much more as a speculative game than as a true financial asset. As economic conditions have worsened and investors have started to feel the pinch, they've been running away from cryptocurrencies, taking their money out as opposed to putting more money in. Burry highlighted this fact very recently by tweeting "are we sure Bitcoin is not just another risk asset in the

Nasdaq." Bitcoin has performed almost exactly as the Nasdaq has done over the past six or seven months. What does this tell us well of course the Nasdaq is home to the big pumped up tech companies in America that are now currently dropping as speculators get out of the market. With Bitcoin almost perfectly mirroring the performance of these stocks it shows you that at this moment in time price movement in cryptocurrencies is also overwhelmingly due to speculation - just like those stocks and currently Bitcoin fails to separate from the pack and hold up as a supposed inflation proof asset. That's the third and fundamental point that has stopped Burry from getting into crypto. At the end of the day cryptocurrencies just by definition have no intrinsic value, they are non-productive assets, and what this means is that the price is only determined by what the next person is willing to pay for them aka speculation and it's not based on underlying cash flows. While you can make that argument as well for gold or cash, these assets do on some level have imputed value because of their importance within the overarching financial system. Gold while non-productive, has been used as a financial asset literally before the time of crisis and the US dollar has the trust of nations around the world as a reserve currency. Bitcoin on the flip side has been around for just over 10 years and really isn't used for anything except speculation. This is

Warren Buffett explaining exactly that point at this year's Berkshire Hathaway annual shareholder meeting; "If the people in this room owned all of the Farmland in the United States and you offered me a 1% interest in it, I'll write your check. This afternoon if you tell me you own 1% of the apartment houses in the United States, I'll write you check. It's very simple. If you told me you owned all of the Bitcoin in the world and you offered it to me for $25, I wouldn't take it because what would I do with it. I have to sell it back to you one way or another, they have the same people but it isn't going to do anything. The apartments are going to produce rental and the farms are going to produce food that explains the difference between productive assets and something that depends on the next guy paying you more than the last guy got and there's only one currency that's acceptable. You can come up with all kinds of things, but in the end this is money anybody that thinks the United States is going to change to where they let Berkshire money replaced theirs, it's out of their mind." That's also Burry's fundamental problem with crypto - it's only ever been used as a gambling machine and its price has always been set by the next most greedy person that has a fear of missing out. He tweeted last year that he saw the greatest speculative bubble of all time in all things, noting that Bitcoin is a speculative bubble that poses more risk than opportunity and the tweet that i mentioned earlier all hype speculation is doing is drawing retail investors in before the mother of all crashes - FOMO parabolas don't resolve sideways - history ain't changed." So far that is exactly what's happened. Crypto is fundamentally speculative and now investors are learning that sometimes when you gamble you lose. He doesn't think this is over anytime soon either. He quoted Tom Siebel in a recent tweet saying "I don't think this is going to be over until everybody swears they'll never own an NFT, never own crypto and they'll never own a technology stock." Burry over the past year has really been quite bearish on crypto and ultimately the reasoning always comes back to the fundamentals. It has no intrinsic value and therefore the price is always the result of the market's appetite for speculation and this makes crypto a pretty easy pass for anyone that has a long-term value mindset. All those YouTubers and fin twits that say Bitcoin will be at a hundred thousand dollars in two weeks or that Ethereum will replace the US dollar in two years - really you just need to ignore them and just invest based off your own conclusions. This is summed up really well in another Burry tweet from last year that was brought to my attention the other week. Burry explains in one single tweet the entire foundation of his investing success. He says "Knowing saves half the battle. Got it? It's not hard. Analyze, think independently, be informed, find the data and a lot that no one else does." If you are able to do that massive losses from speculative bubbles like this bursting are a lot easier to sidestep because chances are you never went anywhere near them to begin with.

Chapter 12 How to Predict Recession using Inverted Yield Curve

It's what everybody's talking about; recession fears are rising, the spread between the two year and the 10-year bond officially inverted for the first time since 2019, a sign that a recession could be on the horizon, it's predicted, recession, recession and recession. I am not about trying to predict recessions and I'm not about trying to time the market. As they say time in the market beats timing the market. But quite bizarrely there is one rather common market metric that has predicted every single recession over the past 50 years and right now it's flashing red once again.

The first time it's done so since 2019 but what is this mysteriously reliable indicator of recessions? Well it's the inversion of the treasury bond yield curve. Before we get into the specifics of the yield curve itself, we have to understand the world of Government bonds. As we know, the US Government spends a lot of money and we definitely know that much is true and when their income isn't sufficient to fund their spending, they sell a bond. A Government bond is a contract between the Government and an investor. The investor loans some money to the Government for an agreed length of time with an agreed annual rate of interest. It's essentially a contract written by the Government and it will say something like "I hereby declare that you should buy this bond from this Government, the Government will pay you a 5% interest payment every year for say ten years at which time the bond will reach maturity and we will give you back your money." This agreement is written on the bond and it doesn't change for the lifetime of it, so if you invested say a thousand dollars into this bond, you would initially be giving the Government a thousand dollars and then each year you would receive fifty dollars in interest until the bond reaches maturity in 10 years time.

At which time the Government will then give you your original thousand dollars back. Here's the tricky bit; after the bonds have been bought from the Government, they are then traded on the open market. You don't have to sell your bonds, you can hold them until maturity and take that promise made to you by the Government, but you may also choose to watch the present market value of your bonds and if the market is offering you a pretty good price for them, then you might choose to sell the bonds and lock in a profit before the maturity date. But why do bond prices fluctuate on the open market? Well from our example above we're outlaying a thousand dollars to get fifty dollars per year for 10 years and then we'll get our thousand dollars back, so we'll have to wait for 10 years to get that full promise. But what if there's clearly a better option out there for investors? What if six months later the Government offers a five-year bond that could make you the exact same amount of money? Well obviously investors are going to be busy buying that fresh bond and they're not going to be super interested in that 10 year bond that you've got, so the market price of your bonds might fall, but here's the crazy thing. The thousand dollar bond you bought is still going to pay out fifty dollars per year for ten years and you're still going to get your one thousand dollars back at the end of it.

Initially this means you signed up for a 5% annual return or a 5% yield, but if the bond price fell down to say 900 on the open market, the bond is still going to pay you $50 a year and you're still going to get back a thousand dollars at the end of the 10 years so this means that if investors decide to buy it at $900 they're going to get a 5.6% yield but that's not all because if they hold under the bond through to its maturity they'll also get a thousand dollars back so they'll get an extra $100. That's the story if bond prices fall but then on the contrary bond prices can also rise. If investors are finding less and less enticing options elsewhere, then your bonds are going to get more and more valuable and their price will rise on the open market. However as the market price rises, the yield of the bond falls because they're only ever going to pay out fifty dollars per year and then return the thousand dollars to you at the 10-year mark. If you pay more on the open market for that deal then that's just bad luck to you. You should have bought them hot off the press when they were cheaper and the yield was higher. That's how bonds work and that's why there's an Inverse relationship between the price and the yield.

The next thing to know is that there are a range of Government bonds out there with different interest rates and different maturities so we can plot these out on a chart where the x-axis shows the time to maturity and the y-axis shows the interest rate and this is called a yield curve.

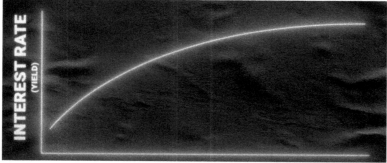

A healthy yield curve will normally take this shape with short-term bonds offering a lower yield than the long-term bonds. In this scenario investors are expecting economic growth and economic growth as we know can lead to inflation which can cause the Federal reserve to raise interest rates thus investors seek a higher yield on those bonds to accommodate this risk. But what we've been seeing lately is a flattening of this yield curve, aka the yield on the long-term bonds has been going down and the yield on the shorter term bonds has been rising. So why would we see this? Well the left-hand side of the yield curve is very much dependent on the FED's decision regarding interest rates.

If the economy is hot and inflation is high, then the Federal Reserve will raise interest rates to make borrowing more expensive to hopefully stop further inflation, and that's what we're seeing happen right now and the FED has already penciled in many more interest rate hikes across the next few years. This raises the yield on the short-term bonds but then on the other side of the chart the yield of long-term bonds reduces because investors see trouble looming in the short term and increasingly want to lock in a set in stone long-term return. This naturally causes a lot of buying of long-term bonds but remember this is a yield curve, so as the long-term bonds are increasingly bought, and the prices rise, the yield lowers because the T's and C's of the bond do not change. Investors are just willing to pay a higher price for the same deal, thus the yield lowers. Overall that's why the yield curve flattens. It's a measure of expectation. If the future looks bright the curve looks healthy. If the future looks sketchy then the curve may flatten or even invert, and right now it's certainly flattening out. But haven't we been hearing in the media that the yield curve has inverted? That still looks like it goes up over time. Instead of looking at all of the bonds of varying maturities, a lot of investors just look at the 10-2 spread. They compare the difference in yield between the 10-year treasury bond and the two-year and when you do that, six months ago we looked absolutely fine. But now it's not looking as great – it's pretty flat.

The chart fluctuates all the time so one day it might be flat and one day it might technically be inverted and we don't know whether right now the curve will be flat or inverted but if we look just last week we did see an inversion of this yield curve which is of course the ticket that news sites needed to plaster it all over their front pages. But why should we care? No one person or indicator is able to accurately predict whether a recession is on the horizon, but weirdly in the case of the 10-2 spread, since this chart started back in 1976, every time it dips negative, the United States has hit a recession shortly after. It's crazy that this literally predicted every single recession for the past 46 or so years and because it so happens this indicator has been very reliable, this is the reason that economists and investors prick their ears up when they hear that right now in 2022 it's just gone negative again. With that said I did just want to discuss some limitations of the 10-2 spread. Firstly, while it has guests the past six recessions, it doesn't magically let how long until the next recession hits, so sometimes it takes a few months and sometimes it takes a few years. Then another factor is that we also haven't seen a sustained period of inversion yet.

As you might expect, if the spread remains negative for a longer period of time, the more likely it is for a recession to occur, but at the moment we're just seeing momentary flutters where it's negative. Then it's also worth remembering that this indicator is just one number and another evidence-based recession indicator is the inversion of the three-month and 10-year treasury bond yield curve, however if we look at that one it's still nowhere near negative. Lastly we have to remember that the stock market and the economy aren't the same thing. An article which has a graph from Truest Advisory Services shows that if you look at the S&P 500 returns in various time periods after the inversion of the two-year and the 10-year treasury yield curve, then the stock market returns have not been a disaster - in fact in five instances the S&P

500 was up double digits just 12 months after the inversion of the yield curve. Overall that's the story of the inverted yield curve. Yes it has been surprisingly good at predicting recessions, however it is just one number and it's worth remembering that it doesn't necessarily spell doom and gloom for the stock market.

Chapter 13 Wheel Options Strategy

2020 is shaping up to be a record year for stock options. Options are the kinds of bets where you can lose everything. Options are riskier than stocks. Options activity hit a record high in 2021. Individuals have often taken to social media. Usually these financial instruments are associated more with the gambling side of the stock market rather than with value investing and in recent years particularly derivatives like options have just gained tremendous popularity as the stock market has been more and more casino affirmative. But what's really interesting is there is a really cool strategy, which includes options, which can be used by the value investor. Surprisingly this option information has not been written about extensively and it's fairly straightforward and it's very cool, so that's what we're going to talk about in this chapter, but if we start at the start first let's just do a quick recap over stock options. There are two main types of options. There are calls and there are puts. These are contracts that are written and sold by one investor and then they are bought by another investor. Let's imagine we've got a stock that's at around say a hundred dollars. Someone writing a call option, might say dear sir madam you have the right but not the obligation to purchase xyz companies shares off of me at any point across the next 12 months for a hundred dollars per share. In this case if the share price rises, then the person that has bought that call option is able to go back to the option writer and say I'm going to exercise this option. They're able to buy the shares off of that person and then sell them on the open market for more. On the flip side someone writing a put option might say dear sir madam you have the right but not the obligation to sell your shares to me at any point across the next 12 months for a hundred dollars per share. In this case this is essentially insurance in case the share price fell lower and if that happened and if the share price did fall lower, then the writer of the put would see themselves taking on that other person's shares for a hundred dollars per share, which is a problem because the share price might have gone lower in the open market. That's calls and puts - they're the basics. If you buy a call you have the right to buy stock at a predetermined price. If you buy a put then you have the right to sell your stock at a predetermined price. If you write a call and sell it to someone they might end up buying your shares off you for a cheaper than market price if the stock prices moved up, and if you write a put and sell it to someone then you might find yourself having to buy the shares at a price that is higher than the current market value. But of course that's the risk right as the person that is writing the option contract. The risk is the stock price moves in the opposite direction of what you need it to. If you wanted to get your hands on one of these very valuable agreements, that will cost you money. You have to buy these put option or call option contracts off of the underwriter. The writer of the option contract will always collect a premium - that always happens, and then the last thing to know is the option contracts do expire. If you've bought an option contract and the share price hasn't moved in your favor during the length of time that contract is open for, then that contract will expire worthless. In that case you've essentially paid for a piece of paper that's worth absolutely nothing - the person that wrote you that contract keeps your premium and doesn't have to do anything else. They don't have to follow through with anything. Now enter Matthew Peterson he is a very funny very cool guy from Austin Texas. He's the one that taught me this options strategy for value investors. He's just a value investor like both you and I but he uses this option strategy to enhance his returns for his fund. His fund's very successful. He started with a hundred thousand dollars he's gotten 18% returns per year for the past 10 years and his funds now with 20 million dollars plus cash inflows. But can options be used effectively by value investors? Absolutely they can. They are used by value investors in fact they're even used and utilized when appropriate by Warren Buffett himself. There's many ways to skin a cat. There's a lot of ways to use these products while a lot of people are out there speculating with these products I tend to flip everything around and I use them in a different manner you can use these contracts to buy securities for less than they cost to the retail investor. What Matt does is he will write a put option contract in order to buy the stock that he already wanted to buy. It's like the best broker you've ever had because now when he enters a position he doesn't have to pay a brokerage fee. He gets paid the premium for writing the put option. What this effectively does is it lowers your cost basis on whatever investment you're making, so it's not speculation at all. It works very well for people that are value minded. As a value investor we want to buy when shares are extremely cheap and so after I've done my analysis especially if there's a lot of volatility in the shares, you can find that these option premiums become systematically overpriced. There is usually a larger demand to purchase these contracts than to sell or underwrite these positions. One really good use of these contracts is looking at the underlying holdings, analyzing the business, figuring out the stock that you want to incorporate into your portfolio, but then checking the option market and if there's a put contract, you could write a cash secured put and get paid a premium just before someone puts you their stocks. That's the basic concept but let's take it one step further and let's really cement how the strategy works by going through a full example and it's an example of a stock that currently sits in Matt's portfolio which is Seritage Growth Properties. Let's say that the Seritage stock price is about 10 and we believe it's worth about 25 or so. Instead of buying it for $10 a share, we can go to the Chicago Board of Exchange, you can write a put contract, committing yourself to buying it for $10, going out seven eight months from now. Today you're able to pick up about 25% of the underlying equity price which means you'd pick up two dollars and fifty cents in premium with a ten dollar commitment to buy and then in our case we hold seven dollars and fifty cents as collateral, so we hold seven dollars and fifty cents, we're paid two dollars and fifty cents - that's our ten dollars in cash and we're just waiting to hopefully buy the shares. The shares will either be in the money or out of the money at the end of the contract. If they're out of the money then we keep the premium and the contracts completed, so we've earned two dollars and fifty cents on our seven dollars and fifty cents of collateral which means we make 33% in seven or eight months which is an astronomical return. Preferably if the shares decline a little bit below the strike, so just below the $10 position we now have the opportunity to buy for $10. If the shares are trading at nine dollars a share the only cost us our net cash outflow is only $7.50 because $2.50 came from the counterpart and that price may not have ever existed in the New York Stock Exchange. So we're able to use these to buy the underlying position for less than the market price and then when the shares do finally appreciate to some expected price - let's call it above 22 and a half. Instead of buying for $10 and making sort of 125 we're buying for 750 now we make 200%. So it's pretty insane but if you have a fairly volatile stock, you can add quite significant extra return on top of just the appreciation of the stock price through selling a put to get in and then selling a call on the way out. If the stock is at 10 and you get paid 2.50 to buy it, then if the shares appreciate to say $22.50, you're going to make a 200% return instead of a 125% return. That is fairly significant but it doesn't always work out as perfectly as what we might like. So here's the four possible outcomes of this approach. The first is that generically your analysis is wrong and the shares go all the way to zero, so instead of buying for 10 and having the shares go to zero and this is a terrible scenario, but you'd buy for seven and a half and the shares go to zero, so on an absolute basis you will lose less, so this is a true risk reduction technique. Ideally the best scenario is the shares decline just below your strike. We want the underlying position so just under $10 if it goes to $9.95 and then the shares are put to us we only pay seven dollars fifty cents and day one we've already made 30% unrealized gain. The third bucket is that the shares are just above the strike price and in that scenario instead of say owning the stock for 10 and having them appreciate to 11 and making 10%, we own it for 10 the contract's finished and in seven or eight months we've made 33% because we've earned the premium $2.50 on top of the $7.50 of our cash collateral. The final example which is the second worst from a professional fund manager perspective it bothers me more than my LPs, our analysis is so correct their shares go from $10 a share all the way to $25 and we only capture a 33% gain. It's not the worst scenario but it's an unfortunate one because we could have made 150% instead we only made 33%. But if you think along those four buckets and you can look at the probabilistic outcome of each and if you're extremely certain that it's not going to go to zero, you can find yourself in a very good situation with this strategy. In all four outcomes obviously you still make money from the premium by selling the put, so there's definitely that risk reduction, no matter what. But obviously the ideal scenario that we want is that we collect the premium, we get the shares, the shares revert back to their intrinsic value over a period of time - that's obviously the ideal outcome. But now let's turn our attention to not just buying but also selling because just like what we're talking about how you can buy a put option to get into the stock, if that stock has then gone up a lot over time, you can then sell a call option to help you get out of the stock and collect a premium on the other end as well. We're talking about Seritage and if Seritage were to then appreciate into something far above the intrinsic value and let's say it ran up to 30 very quickly, we would probably look to exit that position by writing a covered call. We would then write it a little out of the money and out a few months so six or eight months down the line, we might write a call with a strike of 35 and pick up another five dollars because if the shares run from 10 to 30, there will be a lot of euphoria, there will be volatility in the shares and the premiums on the calls will go up considerably. So if we write a call with a strike of 35 and pick up five if the shares go up above 35, somebody will call our shares away from us and our net cash outflow will be 40. If you put both of those parameters in play, we have a scenario where we're buying in for 750 instead of 10, we're selling for 40 instead of 35 and we're picking up pretty significant IRRs on either end and even if this is an eight or a ten year holding period we'll end up enhancing our annualized IRR by 2,3,4,5 % by doing this on either side. At this point it seems pretty clear this is a very intelligent strategy, especially for a value investor that is always going long and really makes sure that they are buying quality companies before they enter into anything. Obviously Matt has implemented this strategy incredibly successfully himself over a long period of time now, but like everything in the stock market, it isn't without its own risks. It would be silly of us not to talk about the risk so let's hone in now what are the risks out there when we're talking about this options approach to value investing. If you consider it as an exposure to your underlying equity, you have the same risk fundamentally as a holder of the underlying equity. There could be a liquidity issue and it could go to zero, however there's all sorts of subtle risks that those engaged in this strategy experience over time. There's corporate events that suddenly alter your strike or there are special dividends that would shift your strike or their spin-offs and mergers. Any sort of activity like this can change the fundamental nature of your contracts. It happens oftentimes very quickly so there are some risks and exposures that are not really seen on the surface. That said, there are some really subtle benefits to implementing the strategy also. One very clear benefit is that in a rational mindset you set something in place that might unwind over the course of six months or a year, even two years, and fundamentally you want to own those shares. When the shares then decline and are suddenly under your strike price in the money and you're now going to be put shares, it's often quite a fearful time because the macro environment might look uncomfortable. The micro environment could look uncertain, but yet you're put the shares and so it's a trigger that forces you to buy when you might feel uncomfortable and it also forces you to sell if you sell a covered call and everything runs up, portfolio managers are not immune to their emotional biases. You can become too greedy and forget to sell, but if you put this in place you are more likely to sell at the right time and buy at the right time. Not only is this a great strategy to help you improve your returns, but it also sets you up with a plan of attack - a rigid plan that you can cling to. So that when the stock gets really volatile maybe it starts falling a lot, it really helps you stick to your evaluation and stick to your trust in your entry and exit points. This led me to one question that I had which I didn't know. Can you literally apply this options strategy to every stock? The shares need to be listed by the Chicago Board of Exchange. The option contracts need to be made available in the public markets through the Chicago Exchange and they just run an algorithm to determine which equities are eligible. It has to do with volume and market cap and a lot of other factors, but ultimately it needs to fit within their parameters to be listed. A lot of foreign firms and even some ADRs are not available, some smaller cap companies are not available, but you can find real nuanced niche situations where volume of some security goes way up and then options are suddenly listed and you have a brief window to write or get involved. you could have a large cap company that becomes a micro cap, but the options still exist because they were available prior to the major decline. So you get some nuanced situations that become pretty opportunistic. Interestingly no you can't always apply this strategy because you need those options to be available. Sometimes the options just aren't available on these stocks and that led me to one last question that I had. Would you always want to implement this strategy or are there times where it doesn't make sense? You need to have some sort of guidelines when you're using this strategy because there are times when the premium is insufficient for the risk. If you're only going to pick up sort of a low single digit annualized IRR on a security, it's probably not worth engaging in this process because you're locking up your collateral for a really low IRR. So you may be better off just owning the underlying security if there isn't sufficient volatility essentially to increase the price and give you an adequate IRR. Your premium needs to compensate you for the fact that you're locking up your capital over a period of time. Sometimes the stock just isn't very volatile and if it's not very volatile, then the options premiums just aren't very enticing. It might just make sense if you just wanted to hold the equity then just hold the equity - just go and buy the stock and maybe adding a 1 or 2% extra return on whatever it might be isn't worth it. But this is a really interesting strategy.

Chapter 14 How To Invest In IPOs (Initial Public Offerings)

In this chapter we're going to be talking about step by step how to participate in an IPO or Initial Public Offering. Before we talk about how to participate in an IPO, it's important to understand what an IPO even is in the first place. An IPO stands for Initial Public Offering and this is the first time a private company issues stock and offers them to the general public. The IPO itself is the final step in a very lengthy process which is referred to as a Company Going Public. If a company is ready to meet the demands of the SEC and has established strong financials, it can file to go public.

The company will then work with an investment Bank who acts as the underwriter for that IPO and this takes many months. It's a very long process. An IPO can be an excellent opportunity for a company to raise capital and potentially accelerate growth because it's a way for them to get new money into the company by issuing shares. Just to give you a visual example of what this looks like, we have a private company which decides to file for an Initial Public Offering. After that, the company hires an underwriter to help navigate the process of the IPO and it's very complicated and takes oftentimes many many months. After that strong marketing materials are created to establish demand as well as gauge interest for the public offering. After that, an IPO date is set with the amount of shares to be offered and a tentative price per share which can fluctuate based on demand and also we have seen in the past some IPOs that were announced that got cancelled because there are times when something will happen with a company in the 11th hour and it can ruin their chances to have an IPO because simply put, nobody wants to buy the shares based on new information coming out. After that, a board of directors are appointed to the company and then other processes for reporting are set in place, because a publicly traded company is held under a lot more scrutiny than a private one and so it's this trade-off that a company has to weigh of do we want to go public and then have to share our financial reporting quarterly and share a lot more information via our prospectus, which could be things that competitors would be able to access and get information that they might have otherwise wanted to keep private. Hence not every company goes public. There's some billion-dollar private companies out there and there's also a lot of large publicly-traded companies. So it's sort of this pro and con thing this trade-off that companies have to determine of whether or not they want to have all of those eyeballs on them and all of those reporting requirements with that advantage of having shares publicly trading, versus keeping it private and not having to share all of that information that their competitors could potentially see. After that the company officially issues shares at the Initial Public Offering. The capital is received as cash and it's recorded on the balance sheet. But how do you participate in an IPO? Well in the past IPOs were reserved for institutions and high net worth individuals. The marketing team for an IPO would go on a road show, they would go to all different investment Bankers, institutional investors and different pension managers and try to sell them those shares at that point in time. Retail investors generally had to wait until a stock reached their financial institution or brokerage account and the downside there is that if there is a lot of a big move with an IPO, oftentimes if a stock goes public it can go much higher or much lower than the Initial Public Offering price immediately and the downside is with most IPOs in the past retail investors wouldn't have an opportunity to get in at the IPO price.

They would only be able to purchase on the market after a new price was settled, based on that supply and demand. Today however anyone can access an IPO with a brokerage such as SoFi and right now very few platforms offer this feature so it is quite unique. Above and beyond just the IPO investing, let's talk more about SoFi and why individuals choose to invest with this app. First of all they have trading with no commissions and a $5 account minimum. They also offer fractional shares via something called stock bits, so if you're looking at stocks that trade for hundreds if not thousands per share, you can rest assured that you can buy a very small amount via a stock a bit or fractional share, that way you don't have to save up all of that money to purchase a whole share. With SoFi you have access to ETFs, stocks, crypto and IPOs. When you open an account with SoFi Invest, you can win up to $1 000. So if you want to check that out and potentially earn up to $1,000 for opening that account check them out.

In addition to that SoFi also offers a lot of other products beyond just investing and you oftentimes aren't going to find this whole suite of products with other financial apps out there. Through SoFi, you can have access to IRA accounts, active or automatic investing, a credit card with cryptocurrency rewards and 2% unlimited cash back cash management account with no transaction fee, early payday and a $100 welcome bonus. They also offer student loan refinancing, personal loans, credit score monitoring and budgeting as well as access to CFAs and career coaching all at no additional cost. More now on the IPO investing with SoFi let's talk about the process. First of all you're in the app you're going to navigate to the Invest tab and then after that you're going to select IPO Investing. After that you're going to click on View Live IPOs and if you want to learn about other opportunities in the future you can click on the button that says Notify Me. But here's the process for IPO Investing with SoFi. Step number one; you're going to see what deals are live and then if any of them interest you you're going to select your IPOs. Step number two; you're going to select how many shares you would like but understand this is not final and it's not guaranteed. You're pretty much saying hey if the opportunity becomes available for me to invest, this is how many I would like to purchase.

Step number three; you're going to confirm your buy order the morning of the IPO. So you're going to want to mark it on your calendar or set a notification in the app and then step number four shares will be allocated the morning of the IPO and you may not receive your whole order due to allocation so hopefully you get part of it - maybe you do get all of it but it all depends on the demand. That being said however there are risks with any investment out there and there are specific risks that do apply to IPO investing. There's many above and beyond this as well but let me cover the basic ones. Any investment out there carries risk and this is very true for IPO investing as well. New companies have less of an operating history and they're far less established. Also IPOs generally have high volatility early on. Just understand there's oftentimes a lot of volatility because the price is ultimately settling as the market determines hey what are people looking to buy this for? What are people trying to sell it for?

And supply and demand justifies a market price over time. As an example of this of how IPO investing can be volatile, we're looking here at Uber stock and this is current as of July 27th 2022. Uber went public in May of 2019 however by September of 2019 the stock was down over 20%. So if somebody had bought it right at the IPO they would have been down 20% or more in the short run. However after that price settled over time we saw that stock move up quite a bit and now it's up over 10% since the IPO as of July 27th 2022. So just to show you there an example of that volatility and the ups and downs that is typical of most IPOs out there. Then for an example of things going in the other direction based on high demand, this was one of the craziest ones out there; Airbnb had an IPO plan that got delayed based on the situation we had earlier in 2020, but then things turned around and then everybody was traveling. So this was a very popular IPO. Airbnb went public in December of 2020 and after just one day the stock was up over a hundred percent. Again that's mostly helpful for those who got in at the early on part of the IPO at the initial IPO price. Retail investors would have to buy it at that 100% inflated price based on the new demand for those shares. That's why it's advantageous to get in on that ground floor of the IPO, before it's on the actual stock exchange. Now Airbnb is up over 97% since it's IPO, but it has cooled off a little bit. So those who bought it after that run-up are potentially down a bit right now. Then for an example here of a nightmare IPO situation of Sundial Growers, they went public in August of 2019 and then by December the company was down 93%.

That would mean if you put a hundred dollars in there you'd have seven bucks left. That's a massive massive loss. So again understand there are massive risks oftentimes associated with IPOs. So tread carefully okay? Also you're going to typically want to have any IPO investing being a very longterm investment because in the short term as you're seeing that price could move any direction. That's an example there of things not working out too well with that IPO. Inside of the SoFi app I'm going to go ahead and give you a quick tour and explain what this app has to offer. You have an invest account and if you click on that, this is where any investments that you have are going to be. It breaks it up in between the individual stock investing as well as the cryptocurrency investing. If you are interested in IPO, you could go to invest, Click on Go to IPO investing and then if you want to be notified of future IPOs, you just click on the blue button that says Notify me. On the home tab you can see your different accounts here and you can see where the balance is and how it's growing over time. It also gives you performance of your different investments. If you do link up with the different spending cards and debit cards and link your accounts, you can also follow spending, look at spending by category and this is all of the budgeting tools that SoFi offers.

They also do free credit score monitoring. If you are interested, you can track the value of your home, tag transactions so many really crazy things you can do within this app. Beyond that here they also show you the performance of any stocks that you've been keeping an eye on. They also show you what are top movers. They're going to show you a utilization of your credit cards if you in fact link those here. There's also the Rewards section where you can claim any reward points that you earn and redeem them. They also have sweepstakes oftentimes going on and there's even a leaderboard if you want to create a social account and track your performance compare it to other people on the app. On the Money tab is where you could open up an account for cash management or if you want it to get a debit card with them to track spending. We have the credit card and they also have the ability to earn cryptocurrency as a reward on your spending if that interests you. We already looked at the investing account and then if you want they also have loans within the app if you want to look at personal loan, student loan refinance or even purchasing a home everything right here within this app.

Chapter 15 How To Research Stocks Using Fundamental Analysis

In this chapter we're going to be talking about how to interpret financial documents for an investment, using the commission-free trading app known as Moomoo. So what exactly are company Financials? Company Financials show relevant business activity and highlight recent performance and they're broken down into three standard reports. Number one is the balance sheet which in my opinion is the most important and that's typically the one I spend most of my time looking at. Number two is the income statement and number three is the cash flow statement and pretty much in that order and I find myself the balance sheet is the most useful the income statement is sort of in the middle and for me the cashflow statement doesn't provide much value to me in terms of the research so if you're going to learn any of these, learning how to interpret a company balance sheet is one of the best research skills that an investor could have.

The balance sheet provides an overview of assets, liabilities and stockholders' equity as a snapshot in time and this is going to be coming out on a quarterly basis. Publicly traded companies are required to report earnings every single quarter and in that reporting they're also providing an updated balance sheet income statement and cash flow statement so when we're seeing a snapshot in time, that could for example be quarter one of 2022 could be that given snapshot of time and that is where that balance sheet and those other documents are referencing back to. Over on Moomoo, you can access this at the snap of a fingers. All you have to do is select a stock, click on financial, click on statements and then balance sheet and it's going to be right there in front of you in the app. The balance sheet highlights how assets are being funded, whether through debt or equity and there's many important metrics to look at such as cash, current liabilities and receivables. One of my favorite things to look at on the balance sheet is that asset to debt ratio and I also like to consider what type of debt this company has. Is it more current liabilities or short-term debt or is this long-term debt that doesn't necessarily have to be paid back in the next 12 months. These are all very useful pieces of information that you're able to gain by interpreting a company balance sheet. The income statement on the other hand highlights a company's revenues and expenses during a particular period of time. For example that might be quarter one of 2022. The income statement is viewed the same exact way. You click on financial click on statements and then select income statement and what you want to be looking for here in general is growing revenues decreasing operating expenses and reducing debt. These are all typically good signs of growth. So if you're looking to understand how fast revenue is growing for a company year over year or quarter over quarter, you're going to find that information over on the income statement. Equally as important as revenue, is the cost of revenue AKA how much money they're spending to go out there and make that money and if you're seeing the cost of that revenue growing faster than the revenue growth, that is something that you just do not want to see. Those are also both very important factors and things to consider when looking at the income statement. That cost of revenue or how much they're spending on going out there and getting that business is referred to as operating expenses. That is what you're going to see when looking at the income statement. If operating expenses are growing at a faster rate than revenue, that would be a bad sign. The last one is the cash flow statement this measures how well a company generates cash to pay its debt obligations fund its operating expenses as well as fund different investments. Again it's viewed the same way, you click on financial click on statements and then you click on the cash flow statement. It's important to analyze cash flow statements in conjunction with the income statement because these work together to paint a bigger picture.

The cash flow statement provides a summary of cash inflows and outflows of a company. So if you want to follow the path of money coming in and money going out, that's all going to be shown through that cash flow statement and cash flows can be positive while net income is negative so that is another tricky thing there to look out for. There's a lot of creative accounting that goes on with financial documents and you also run into GAAP versus non-GAAP figures. GAAP is the Generally Accepted Accounting Principles. If you're using different numbers as comparison metrics, you would always want to compare GAAP numbers to GAAP numbers or non-GAAP numbers to other non-GAAP numbers. But I always follow the GAAP numbers the Generally Accepted Accounting Principles that are enforced by the SEC and other regulatory agencies. Right off the bat here what exactly is Moomoo?

This is an advanced trading platform that obviously offers access to commission-free trading but it's available to stocks as well as options and ETFs. Moomoo is based in the Silicon Valley in California. However Moomoo Inc is an indirect wholly owned subsidiary of a larger parent company based out of China called Futu Holdings Limited. Despite the fact that they are based out of China that parent company this is still an SEC registered broker-dealer that is a member of FINRA and SIPC. So in layman's terms what that means is that Moomoo has the same exact regulation as any other peer operating in the United States. As far as the reason behind why people choose Moomoo, it typically comes down to the features because at the end of the day commission-free trading is available everywhere now and that's not really much of a differentiating factor. But beyond that, there's a few things that Moomoo does offer. First of all free Level 2 market data and real-time quotes. Beyond that, they also offer advanced charting and research tools, customizable dashboards, stocks, ETFs options as well as a free stock incentive at the sign-up. So if you want to check out Moomoo and get a ton of free stocks in the process pretty much all you have to do is open up an account and put a very small amount of money in there and they're pretty much just going to hand you a bunch of free stocks. The question becomes, using these financial statements what exactly are the key indicators to look for? Well I'm going to give you a few and these are some of my favorites. First of all earnings per share tells you how much the company earns in profit per share. For every share that you own, that is your corresponding amount of earnings based on the total earnings of the company. Beyond that, return on equity is another good metric to look at as well as return on assets. The current ratio is very helpful too to determine if the company is going to be in a bit of a cash crisis because the current ratio shows you the current assets divided by current liabilities and that simply means the amount of money that they have in cash or readily convertible to cash in the next month, compared to the debt obligations that they have to pay back in the next 12 months. For example if a company had a million dollars of current assets and then $1.2 million of current liabilities, at this point in time even have enough money for those debts that are going to come due later on sometime in the next 12 months so looking at that current ratio is a really good metric to understand if there's going to be any cash constraints on this company in the next 12 months. After that, looking at net margin which is simply taking your net profit, divided by total revenue it's another great indicator to be able to understand but there's hundreds and hundreds more above and beyond that. What I recommend doing here instead of trying to learn all of these at once, you start with one, you do more research on what that indicator is and then you look at different companies out there. If you want you can use Moomoo, that way you don't have to change between different apps and then once you fully understand one of these key indicators then you build upon that and you add another indicator. However I do have to warn you to be careful of going into too much detail because there is such thing as that analysis paralysis where if you're simply looking at too much information, a lot of it is going to contradict other information and you might just get totally scrambled and end up making no decisions whatsoever. So don't overdo it but find that fine line there of doing enough research where you can make your decision, but don't go too far into it to where you contradict yourself and you get that analysis paralysis. Overall, the indicators provide you with a glimpse into the company's financial health. A good key indicator should be taken with a grain of salt. For example tech companies typically feature higher debt. Established companies typically have more consistent cash flows, so there's different traits or characteristics of different types of stocks out there. For example they're looking at tech or growth stocks, versus more blue chip or value stocks. Key indicators are often used to compare companies within the same sector. For example if you're looking at the PE ratio, that is something where you would compare the PE ratio of two companies within the same sector or industry. Comparing a company like Exxon Mobil and Facebook makes absolutely no sense. There's totally different ways that those businesses are being valued. Facebook is being valued a lot based off of their DAU and MAU and their active users. Exxon Mobil is being valued based on so many other factors such as gas stations or distribution channels. That's not a fair comparison and it's not a useful comparison to look at the PE of Exxon Mobil compared to Facebook. On the other side of the coin it would make sense to compare the PE ratio of Facebook to Twitter and Twitter to Snapchat, just the same as it would make sense to compare the PE ratio of Exxon Mobil to Chevron and Chevron to BP, but you just don't mix the two and compare PE ratios or any other key indicators between completely different sectors or industries. Moomoo makes this incredibly easy with the Stock Compare feature. Stock Compare can be found by visiting the financial tab moving over to indicators and then clicking on Stock Compare and this is going to allow you to quickly compare indicators among two to three different companies that you add yourself. For example if we created this comparison looking at Tesla versus Toyota Motors. Tesla currently has a net margin of 4.47% while Toyota has a net margin of 8.39. So what exactly does this mean? Well that means that for every dollar of revenue Tesla earns about 4.47 cents, meanwhile Toyota earns just about double somewhere around there - maybe not quite double at 8.39 cents. You could look at that and create a comparison chart and if you wanted to you could throw another automaker in there may be Ford and then straight across the line you can look at return on equity, return on assets, gross margin, debt to asset ratio, net margin and just be able to look at it very quickly set up comparisons and do tons of research in a very short consolidated period of time. Obviously looking at the app, there's tons of different features to Moomoo and a lot of them are going to be above and beyond the scope of what we cover in this chapter but will mention a few things just to get a general idea of all of the different features available on Moomoo. In order to get to those financial documents you have to scroll all the way to financials. This is where we're going to get the bulk of our information researching this company. There's a lot of different things in here that you can look at in terms of different indicators, revenue composition, where their money is coming from - all kinds of stuff like that. Earnings per share financial estimates et cetera et cetera. It also shows you line charts, showing the trends on the balance sheet, the cash flow statement and the income statement and how they are changing. But in particular this is what we're curious about is those actual statements. So if you want to view those, you click on the statements button and then you click details next to the statement that you're looking to view. For example this is the number one concern among investors is that Genius Brands right now is simply not focused on revenue because they're building out a children's cartoon app and they're investing a ton of money into content for that. So right now revenue is negligible and there's not much to speak of. Whereas in quarter one of 2021 they had about $1.06 million of revenue. However the year over year growth is 217.94%. We talked about that cost of revenue being something that you have to watch out for. You don't want to see that growing faster than total revenue. We only saw a cost of revenue increased by 9.21%. Meanwhile total revenue increased over 200%. So that in my opinion is a good sign. Next we'll jump over to the balance sheet and take a look at what's going on here. Genius Brands is an absolute cash cow. Believe it or not right now Genius Brands is sitting on $143.61 million cash in the Bank, using that money to buy media assets and just do things to grow the overall business. Right now they're sitting on a mountain of cash with minimal debt which is something I like to see with my investments. Overall looking at the metrics we see cash and cash equivalents but you want to scroll down to the debts just to have a general idea. In this case the total assets for this company comes in at 205.79 million. But if you scroll down, total debts or total liabilities are just $30 million. So this company has more than $6 in the Bank for every dollar of debt that they have and that is something I like to see in my investments. This is similar to Google or Facebook or some of these other cash cow companies. The difference being that those are close to trillion dollar companies and this is being valued at 1/2 of a billion dollars right now. There's a lot more to Genius Brands. Don't just buy it based on the balance sheet, do your own research. I'm just strictly using this stock for demonstration purposes of what we're looking for within these financial documents. That's typically what I look for there is total assets total debt, do they have a lot more assets than debt? Yes they do. That's a good sign to me. So then we're going to lastly jump over and take a look at the cash flow statement. I very rarely even look at this but I am just going to show you a general idea of what you have available to you. This is the financial document that I have the least knowledge of and I just simply don't use it that often but this is where you would navigate to if you want to interpret that cash flow statement. That is how you can research important financial documents and how to use Moomoo if you want to do it all within one easy to use commission-free investing app. As mentioned it might be a little bit more going on than a complete beginner might want but if you have been trading for a while and you're looking for a brokerage that simply just has more to offer, Moomoo is a great option to consider.

Conclusion

Congratulations on completing this book! I am sure you have plenty on your belt, but please don't forget to leave an honest review on Amazon. Furthermore, if you think this information was helpful to you, please share anyone who you think would be interested of entrepreneurship as well.

About The Author

Will Weiser is a successful serial entrepreneur, born in New York in 1961. Will has graduated for Business Management in New York 1989, but only started his first company 12 years later in 2001 selling t-shirts on the street. Will made his first million dollar in 2014 and then his first 10 million by 2017. Will's total portfolio has reached $76 Million by the end of 2021 and keeps growing. Will got married with Kate Hirsh, and having three beautiful children; Jack, Tony and Andrew. Together with his wife they both looking after several businesses they own including several Retail Businesses and Beauty salons.